M000289702

PRAISE FOR
A LEGACY OF FAITH

Jesus prayed these words recorded in John 14, "I tell you the truth, anyone who believes in me will do the same works I have done, and even greater works, because I am going to be with the Father." We see the fulfillment of the prayer Jesus prayed written in the pages of this memoir. Doug and Debi have lived a life of radical faith and authentic devotion. They live the words they preach. They have laid their lives down to walk in the way set before them, and the fruit of their sacrifice is evident. As a part of their community for decades, I heard these stories shared time and time again. I even lived in some of them. These experiences never lost their impact. The stories have inspired thousands around the globe already, as I know they will continue to do for generations through these pages.

Jessi Cieply
Missionary, Worship Leader

'Go therefore and make disciples of all nations....' Debra Tunney has laid out a journey that every Christian can and should go on. From unbeliever to believer to disciple to evangelist, she captures the fears and joys of learning how to hear God's voice and trust in Him. Her testimonies of God's miracles in her life and in the lives of others practically shout of God's love for us, all the while giving all the glory to Him!

Christine St Cyr
President, Central New Hampshire Employment Services

This book chronicles the lives of Doug and Debi Tunney, two lives given over to God. Doug and Deb founded Youth With A Mission Centers in Pittsburgh, Boston, and Philadelphia. They have had enough experiences, if told in detail, to fill ten books. The story is real; they tell of their triumphs and their downfalls. They reveal their brokenness and God's healing. When I think of them, a quote by the Apostle Paul always comes to mind, "I am not ashamed of the Gospel." They remind me of cream on the top of milk. Every time they got knocked down, they would rise back to the top—demonstrating God's faithfulness. I highly recommend that you read this book. If you do, you will be encouraged to walk with God, challenged to have a heart for the lost without Christ, and motivated to never give up on your dreams.

Ken Barnes
Author, *The Chicken Farm and Other Sacred Places* and
***Broken Vessels;* Former Missionary with Youth With A Mission**

This book is one of the most encouraging books you will ever read. Doug Tunney is the 'purest' evangelist I have ever known or read. Doug, thanks for writing about your walk with the Lord all these years.

Pastor John Derrico
The Christian Center Church

Doug and Debi's stories of faith are some of the most amazing testimonies I have ever heard. Just being around them over the years has inspired me to share the gospel more and trust God for greater things. Reading their book, "Legacy of Faith," gives hope to what God can do through ordinary people when we yield our lives to an Extra-Ordinary God!

Gwen Bergquist
Youth With A Mission, Destiny by Design

Attempt great things for God, and you will accomplish great things for God. Doug Tunney shared this message with me as a young man just starting out in ministry. Doug and Debi Tunney have lived out this message in a hundred different ways and in a thousand different settings. *A Legacy of Faith* shares the amazing story of a young couple hearing and following the voice of God, putting the

Gospel of Jesus Christ above all else. As you read, YOU will want to attempt some great things for God yourself!

Tom Hollis
COO, CornerStone Television Network

Doug and Debbie are biblical practitioners! They are exceptions to the norm of living nominal life. There are few people I know personally who exhibit applied principled life. Doug and Debi are among those very few people! I have often secretly desired to be like them, as they are like Jesus to people. They are among the first to admit to mistakes and the first to align with the word of God with literally no compromises. This book will challenge us to live life to a higher worth as they do so well.

Sam Dharam
YWAM Asia Pacific Eldership Team

As I reflect on this insightful memoir, I gain a deeper understanding of God's magnificent plans for his children and his limitless power to change the world through those who follow him. I am also blessed with a deeper sense of gratitude and respect for Deb and Doug Tunney, my eternal friends.

Dr. Nick Palmieri
Author, *Strength Renovation: Rebuilding Faith Communities*
Retired Professor

Anyone who has had the pleasure of knowing Doug and Deb Tunney knows they are the real deal. Their lives reflect adventurous faith, selfless love, and a deep passion for Jesus. The stories in this book will encourage and inspire you to deepen your own walk with Christ. As people, God has wired us for stories. The stories Deb shares draw us in and make us want to say, "More, please." Enjoy, and get ready for a great read.

Becky Toews
Author, *Between the Lamp Posts* and *Keep Your Lamp Burning*

A LEGACY OF FAITH

OUR GOD STORIES FROM FAMILY,
MISSIONS AND MINISTRY

Debra Tunney

Worldwide Publishing Group
HOUSTON, TEXAS

PART SIX

DEDICATION

&

A WORD TO OUR FAMILY

WE WANT TO dedicate this story to our family. You all bring joy and purpose to our lives every day. Your lives inspire us as we see these values lived out to the fullest: family, integrity, hard work, courage, and sacrificial love.

To our children:

- Rachel and Aaron
- Bethany and Chuck
- Douglas and Amanda
- Jeremy and Kandia
- Brian and Jennifer

To our grandchildren: Emily Estelle, Anna Olivia, Ethan Hutton, Owen Harrison, Ellie Jane, Charles Warren, Luke Coleman, Schenley Lydia, Adalyn Felicity, Levi Patrick, Layna Elise, LilliAnne Mackenzie, Maycee Evalyn Joy, Maggie Caelan, Evan Henry, and Miranda Elizabeth.

While each person begins their own faith walk, there is a legacy of faith that is yours. Paul encouraged Timothy to fan into flame the gift of God. He reminded him of the legacy of faith instilled by his grandmother Lois and his mother Eunice (2 Timothy 1:6).

And how from infancy you have known the Holy Scriptures,
which are able to make you wise for salvation. Therefore, through
faith in Christ Jesus.
2 Timothy 3:15 NIV

Greatly desiring to see you, being mindful of your tears, that I
may be filled with joy, when I call to remembrance the genuine
faith that is in you, which dwelt first in your grandmother Lois
and your mother Eunice, and I am persuaded is in you also.
Therefore, I remind you to stir up the gift of God which is in you
through the laying on of my hands.
2 Timothy 1:4–6

We began this book intending to capture stories from our lives for *you*. Our journey of faith is the greatest treasure we could give to you. We wanted to show you what it is like to abandon your life for God's purposes and make knowing Him the highest priority of your life.

Cape Ann Camping was where we brought our pop-up camper for the weekend and reminisced about our lives. What did we want you to know about God and life?

We knew you would sometimes face challenges that would scare you. At times, you would wonder if you had it in you to keep going; at other times, you would wonder if God was there or if He cared for you while He was running the universe.

While we tried to walk with you through your lives and do what Deuteronomy says—talk about the Lord in the everyday moments of life—we realized those moments would someday fade, and you might forget.

Fix these words of mine in your hearts and minds; tie them as reminders on your hands and bind them on your foreheads. Teach them to your children, talking about them when you sit at home and when you walk along the road, when you lie down and when you get up. Write them on the doorframes of your houses and on your gates.
Deuteronomy 11:18–20 NIV

You shall teach them diligently to your children, and shall talk of them when you sit in your house, when you walk by the way, when you lie down, and when you rise up.
Deuteronomy 6:7

With that in mind, we made a list—a "this is important" list—of events containing stories of God's faithfulness and utter trustworthiness. It was a list of what we knew for certain about His character and the lessons we had learned over the past fifty years.

It was important that we told the truth, the best we could remember, realizing that time bends our memories a bit. So, we reached out to friends and fellow travelers along the way and verified the details when possible. Our list was 453 moments, people or life lessons, and we worked to bring this book to you.

We made sure we didn't sugarcoat or whitewash the struggles. You need to see authentic faith, and that includes stumbles, overcoming obstacles, and the times we made decisions that were not the best. We can't keep you from making your own mistakes, but there is always a second chance, redemption, and forgiveness. Having wise counselors who will tell you the truth and stick with you when your life gets messy is important.

Not every one of those 453 moments made it here, but the ones that *did* reflect the true telling of our story. In Joshua, chapter 4, God instructed Joshua to build a memorial of twelve stones on the land and twelve stones in the riverbed of the Jordan River. They had just crossed over the river as they began their journey into the Promised Land, where giants awaited them. A failed generation had preceded them. The Lord wanted to give them a reminder of his faithfulness. He said that in the future, their children would ask what the pile of stones meant. Those teachable moments would be the way Joshua's generation could pass on courage, passion, and faith to the next generation.

The pile of rocks in the riverbed would only be visible in times of need when drought would bring the water level low, and resources would be at a bare minimum. Even then, God wanted them to remember their journey from Egypt through the wilderness to the Promised Land. Remembering is powerful. The Scriptures encourage us to remember hundreds of times.

You are the most important of all the things we treasure in our lives. We never accumulated much earthly treasure. Poppy has his many clocks, and I have some family dishes. But on the wall in the hall of our home, we have your photos. It is a daily reminder of what is most important to us. When guests come, we never always show you off to them. If they would listen, we would tell them brief stories about you, how much we love you, and the special things you are doing.

Poppy and I hope you read these words. We hope someday your children and their children will ask you what these stories mean, and you will have treasures of your own to add to them.

A NOTE TO THE READER

KATE MOTAUNG wrote this for her memoir, *A Place to Land: A Story of Longing and Belonging*. And I couldn't have said it better.

All writing is a challenge, but memoir proves to be a particularly slippery genre simply because of the nature and frailty of the human memory. I've done my best before God to offer an accurate reflection of the events described in the pages that follow, realizing, of course, that my recollection is fallible and faltering. Some names have been changed out of respect and privacy for the people mentioned.

INTRODUCTION

A good man leaves an inheritance to his children's children.
Proverbs 13:22

CAN ORDINARY smooth stones in the hands of God reach a generation? Saturday mornings are often full of adventure for us. Our hobby of searching for treasures at yard sales frequently takes us to interesting places and people's stories. We watch for signs directing us to sales as we drive through neighborhoods. One morning, we pulled up to an estate sale; a family was closing a beautiful estate for a loved one. They were selling some items and preserving the treasures for the heirs. Walking through a home that is being dissolved is sobering. You feel like an intruder.

I wondered, "Who were these people? What were their families like? What were their dreams? Did they settle their regrets? What did they leave behind?"

The contents of their home gave clues about what they enjoyed, the treasures they collected, the possessions they valued, and the people they loved. There were photos on the walls: baby photos, graduations, and family gatherings with smiling people. Stories lingered here—traces of what made their lives meaningful.

I hope this book will be like a walk through our lives and tell a story of faith—our hearts' surrender to God and our unrelenting pursuit of His destiny for our lives. It is an intentional collection of whom we loved, what we valued, and stories of God's faithfulness. These are our treasures, stored up for the next generation. Our love for God has been the defining motivation of our lives. Our relationship with Him has been the center. Jesus is our greatest treasure, and our quest to know Him has given purpose and direction to our story.

This legacy is the greatest inheritance that we can give to our children's children. What our children have seen in us has been their greatest teacher.

In 2 Timothy 1:5–6, Paul encourages Timothy and exhorts him to fan into flame the faith that is in him and that also lived in his grandmother, Lois, and his mother, Eunice. Bringing our faith to the next generation is a gift and a challenge. Our lives can be a signpost that helps our children open their hearts to know the Lord.

Every life story includes struggle. We want to share the struggles that we faced, the faithfulness of the Lord to meet us in the darkest of times, and how we grew through adversity. Our lives have been tested, and our faith has grown. We have faced disappointments and detours, injustice, and our own limits and failings. As they see God's love and grace toward us, we hope it will strengthen others.

Christians are drifting away from being committed to a local church and relationships with other believers. Sometimes people walk out of the doors of churches because of hurt and hypocrisy.

But instead of walking away, we found the grace to forgive and be forgiven. The Church has no lone rangers. We have also experienced the love and support of fellow believers and the strength that comes from living with a shared purpose, vision, and service. Here are thoughtful reasons behind our commitment to the sanctity of life.

We chose to be activists and to bring compassion and truth to those struggling with unplanned pregnancies. So often, the responses to unplanned pregnancies are angry, harsh, and end rather than begin communication. We prefer a response that is quiet and kind, which will lead to understanding and practical support.

Our involvement in founding pregnancy centers came from our hearts. We were burdened with concern for the women, the men, and the babies. We hope to leave an inheritance of hope and life as we continue to speak up for the unborn. Our choice was to be a compelling positive response to a culture of death that has left millions of hearts broken and regretful. A generation of children has been lost because they were an inconvenience.

Our deepest desire is to leave a spiritual heritage for our children and their children so that they might set their hope in the Lord, remember His works, and keep His commands. Deuteronomy tells us how to engage our family. We are to talk about it, live it out before them, and invite them in as we live out our faith in the everyday moments of our lives. We must face our mistakes and trust God for the grace to overcome them. Some things have made a big difference for us and our children.

Recently, I walked two of my young granddaughters along a stream. The edges were lined with smooth rocks; well-worn with the seasons of life: the rising of spring water, the summer droughts and the winter snows. The passage of time had left some smooth stones.

The girls raced to the water's edge and began throwing rocks into the stream.

"Come see what you can do with these stones," I said.

I gathered a handful of perfectly molded stones, ready to be sent across the water. I told them, "Hold them in your hand and sling them; watch how they skip and how each touch on the stream creates a splash and ripples."

They took the challenge and joyfully began slinging. They filled the stream with ripples.

It made me think about our lives. I realized we have been stones in God's hands, tossed with purpose and making many ripples that have touched thousands of lives. This book will capture some of our stories and hopefully inspire others to spend their lives making ripples for God's glory.

A SMOOTH STONE

A smooth stone in the hand of a mighty God
A lake, calm and quiet
Early in the morning, the sun rises over it, peaking over the pine trees
that surround it
The surface of the water begins to steam
Before the world awakens for the day
Before the bugs start buzzing
Before the ducks come out of their nests
Before the birds sing their morning song
A man steps up to the shore
He picks up a stone and slings it over the calm, still, and glassy water
The stone is smooth, rounded perfectly, and fits perfectly in the hand
of the thrower to do exactly what He intended it to do
The stone glances on the water once, twice, three times, four,
then five
It does not slow down
It continues...
Six, seven, eight, nine, and ten
Then, finally, the energy in the stone dies
It falls into the lake, never to be seen above the water again
But with each skip, the stone left a mark, a ripple, far-reaching and
unforgettable
With each strike, it went further
It made a new impact, a new adventure
And it accomplished the intended purpose of the Thrower
He stands at the shore, looks out over the water, and watches as the
ripples extend all the way to the shoreline

With an approving smile, He looks over the water, and the world around comes to life

Let us be that smooth stone in the hand of God, ready to do His work in line with His will, unafraid of where He will send us but trusting Him in obedience to do the work and to follow the path that He has in mind for us.

- Colin Lockwood

PART ONE

California Fellowship at California University

California, Pennsylvania

CHAPTER 1

HAIR, LET THE SUNSHINE IN

MY PARENTS dropped me off at Kitt Hall, a freshman dorm, with a suitcase of clothes and some homemade brownies. Then, after a tight hug and an emotional goodbye, they drove away, leaving me on my own at seventeen.

I was at California State College with thousands of other freshmen during a time of social unrest. The year 1969 was one of upheaval and historical significance. Richard Nixon was the president, the Vietnam War was raging, and men were landing on the moon for the second time. Many students were "in school" to avoid the draft. The assassinations of Robert Kennedy and Martin Luther King the year before had shaken our nation to its core.

From my first moment on campus, I knew I had stepped into a radically different world than the one I had grown up in. Loud psychedelic music and pot smoke filled the halls. My father had insisted that I attend college there despite my choice of Geneva College. I came with anger. The hostile environment of the campus fueled my resentment into deep bitterness.

My faith began when I was eight years old. I attended Sunday school at the Webster Presbyterian Church, where I heard Bible stories and memorized scripture. Dora Ritchie was my Sunday school teacher. She was a kind elderly woman, faithful, and dedicated to the church and our Sunday School class. I always asked questions, but many were left unanswered. Unfortunately, my unanswered questions turned into unbelief.

Anti-war, anti-authority, and anti-religion were the cries of my generation in 1969. My professors, who often came to class high on drugs and social revolution ideas, expanded this worldview. It was a lot of pressure for my seventeen-year-old intellectual mind. After a few weeks, I fit in with the drumbeat of social change. A new religion smothered my childhood faith, a total rejection of "old ways." I traded in the outdated, distant God of biblical myths and restrictions for a new god of existentialism.

However, this new world didn't bring the fruit of peace into my life. On the contrary, I felt more confused and lost. Everyone in my life was so messed up. My father was an alcoholic. My professors were living out their philosophies, and many of them were divorced or in the middle of broken relationships. They were often high on drugs. The path they were on led many into more confusion.

My new friends on campus strode headlong into this wild atmosphere. Some failed their classes, and many lived day to day for parties or protests. Not one of them had anything that looked like peace. Broken hearts and dreams replaced the idealism that they came with.

It was Led Zeppelin and bell bottoms, protest signs, and late-night conversations about what was wrong in the world. I took a half step into things that could have brought a lot of pain into my life. The Lord protected me from those consequences. I went from academic honors in high school to barely passing in college. My underlying anger and confusion affected every area of my life.

"This is the dawning of the Age of Aquarius. Let the sunshine in." The music blared as I sat in the Nixon Theater in Pittsburgh in the spring of 1971 at a performance of the Broadway play "Hair." Marijuana

smoke filled the hall. Hair pushed the envelope of what was acceptable for moral entertainment. It was a statement of rebellion in a time of political upheaval and international crisis, with the Vietnam War raging and college students protesting the state of the nation.

Jeff, the boyfriend I came with, was lost. As the performance went on, I thought about my life. Who had the answers to life? It was very clear. No one had it together.

The only peace I had known was from my walk with God. The only wisdom I saw was in the scriptures. The only hope I saw was in believers' lives. As the "Age of Aquarius" was blasting, I gave my life back to the Lord. I whispered, "Lord, if you are real, please help me, forgive me, and bring me back to yourself." That was it. A simple prayer in an unlikely place rekindled the commitment I made as an eight-year-old child.

It was a step of faith, but not blind faith. It was a simple decision to turn from confusion and darkness to a fresh path, one I knew as a child.

On the ride back to my dorm, I made a profession of faith to Jeff. "I decided tonight about my life." He looked surprised. "And that is?"

"I have decided to follow Jesus." I was surprised at the confidence I felt. My words seemed to strengthen the resolve I felt.

"Okay, I can get into that too, no problem." His response wasn't about a conviction but more about keeping our relationship.

"I am very sure that it won't be working like that. I hope you want to follow Jesus. But that will not work for our relationship to continue."

Breakups are never easy. This one was right for me. When I closed the car door, I knew I would never see him again. He was a part of the life that I was walking away from.

I talked about the Lord with my friends the next day. I knew I had found the truth again. I wanted to tell everyone in my world about it.

My dorm room was always filled with friends dropping by to talk. The focus of those conversations now became Jesus.

"What happened to you at Hair?" This was a question I answered daily. Confusion and unrest were gone, and in their place was a settled peace. The prayer I whispered in my heart was real, and a transformation had taken place. I didn't have answers to all my questions, but I had decided to follow Jesus. There was no turning back for me now.

I knew a few things for sure. First, I had to shut the door on all the thoughts and relationships that would draw me back. All the things that belonged to that life—books, music, places, and all that tied me to a relationship with my ex-boyfriend. I knew that on this new path, I had to let go of reminders and distractions.

Months before, I had stopped in to see Ginny Keteles, who was the leader of the Intervarsity group. Even though I wasn't following Jesus, I was still attracted to Christians and wanted to engage in faith-based and kingdom-based conversations with them. Most of the time, I resisted their faith, but I was drawn to connect with them. Ginny's roommate was not a believer. She later told Ginny that I was a lost cause and would never become a believer.

I looked for Ginny over the next few days. She invited me to the Intervarsity meeting. Most of the students there were seniors and would be gone at the conclusion of the semester. I didn't click well with them. That was the only group of believers I knew on campus.

When the fall came, I was in a new dorm with new friends. My conversations were often about my faith. Girls would gather in my room to hang out. Most conversations would end up talking about Jesus. Soon, there were new believers in the group. We went to The California Fellowship (now Intervarsity). Our faith was contagious.

Donna lived in Stanton Hall. She passed by me one afternoon as I was in the lobby with a few of my friends. She said, "Hey, I heard you were into Jesus. We should talk about that sometime." She didn't seem like the type who would be interested. But I remembered Ginny's friend's comment that I would never become a Christian. I realized God knows people's hearts, and we can never know what He is doing in someone's life.

A few weeks later, Donna joined us at Christian Fellowship. I was a resident assistant, and late at night, he would come in and sit with me for hours, talking about Jesus. Soon after, she decided to follow Him. This happened repeatedly as girls who I never thought would be interested in Jesus became solid believers.

> *Do not be amazed that I said, 'You must be born again.' The wind blows where it wishes. You hear its sound, but you do not know where it comes from or where it is going. So, it is with everyone born of the Spirit.*
> John 3:7–8 BSB

CHAPTER 2

JESUS PEOPLE

"JESUS IS alright with me."

I could hear the singing as soon as I opened my car door. I looked at my notepad where "The Millers" was written in bold letters. The name on the mailbox was the correct address for the Jesus People meeting.

Marie met us at the door with a kind, welcoming smile and invited us in. Ken, another first-timer, and I found places to sit on the floor. People squished together to make room for us.

"Cup of tea?" she asked.

I nodded.

Spice tea, Jesus music, and an overfilled living room are my powerful memories from that first night at the Millers' residence. Pastor Dan Sommers was the teacher. Even though he sat on the floor with the rest of us, he obviously was from another generation. The bell bottoms and hippie-haired Jesus people, combined with a clean-cut Baptist preacher, made for an odd gathering.

Ricky put down his guitar. The room was still. Pastor Dan began reading 1 John 2. As if orchestrated, everyone leaned in to listen as he read. The Bible was alive; every word was filled with wisdom and clarity.

My mother made a promise to God when I was gravely ill before my second birthday. She vowed that if God spared my life, she would dedicate me to Him and do her best to help me know Him. She kept that promise, and wherever we lived, she took me to Sunday school. As a result, I grew up memorizing scripture and singing Christian songs. I had God's Word planted deep in my heart, waiting for this time when the Holy Spirit would bring water and make the scriptures alive to me.

"Glad you stopped by tonight!" Marie hugged me on the way out the door. "When did you begin to follow Jesus? Let's sit down so you can tell me your story. Do you want another cup of tea?"

"When I was eight years old, my father and grandmother were having a very loud argument. I was trying to fall asleep. Their fight kept me awake," I told her after we found a place to sit.

"They were arguing about whether the age of accountability was eight or twenty. I didn't know why they were discussing this, but my heart was moved, and I thought, 'I'm eight. What if eight is when you should give your life to God?' As the loud words continued downstairs, I whispered a prayer in my bed, 'Jesus, I give you my life.'"

"Very cool!" Marie affirmed. "What happened that brought you here?" That was a story for a longer visit, and Ken and I committed to returning the following week.

Pastor Dan showed up each week with the next chapter of 1 John. My childhood scriptures were now becoming a foundation of faith for me. My whole life was being transformed by the Holy Spirit.

CHAPTER 3

JESUS IS JUST ALRIGHT WITH ME

"WOW, THIS is such a cool sculpture!"

I glanced up from my Teaching Reading textbook. His voice boomed in the silent library.

"Thanks, but I am not an artist," I whispered timidly. "I'm studying how to teach art to children."

As he walked away, something lingered with me. Something in his expression, something in his eyes, suggested a longing for a friend. He didn't introduce himself; however, there was a lasting impression. I remembered him.

Weeks later, our small intervarsity group met in the upper room of the Presbyterian Church. For months, we had been gathering for Bible study and fellowship. The same handful of students met each week. There were no recent visitors because we had become isolated and irrelevant. God did not call the church to hide under a bushel (as the Little Light of Mine song went).

There was a stirring in our spirits to bring the Gospel to our campus. The seventies were a time of unrest in the world; war, racial tension, the hippie movement, drugs, and the sexual revolution marked that time. Those things reflected the fallen state of man. Our response was to take a step out of our isolated small group and venture out onto our campus to share the Gospel. That first day out was intimidating and uneventful, with a bit of persecution added to it.

Nick, one guy in the group, had a long day of closed doors, closed minds, and closed hearts, along with some cynical rejection, that left him exhausted and not thrilled about repeating the experience. On his way back to the dorm, he mulled over the day and speculated on what he could have done better. Nick noticed a guy walking his way.

"What the heck, one more!"

Nick shot a prayer to heaven and caught up to this stranger.

"Praise the Lord!" That wasn't a subtle greeting, and there was no response. Instead, the stranger looked away and walked faster.

"Hey, what are you doing tonight? Do you want to come to a Bible study we are having at the Presbyterian Church?"

Those words stopped him mid-stride. He wasn't interested in Bible study or going to church, but someone was reaching out to him and inviting him to connect.

"I'll try to make it!"

That night, our group talked about how our first day of outreach. Most of us had uneventful days. Nick concurred, but said he had one friendly conversation and hoped to see the guy tonight. Our meeting was interrupted when the door was nudged open, and to my surprise, the guy I met in the library peeked in. "Is this the Bible study place? I'm Doug."

We greeted him with an over-the-top welcome, and I now knew his name. Maybe he was a believer. During the next few weeks, Doug showed up. He was the first one to arrive and greet us all. He contributed to the conversation. He seemed to fit in. When Nick asked him to set up the chairs the next week, he hesitated. He was always early. He seemed eager to help. We didn't know what was going on in his mind. He was dipping his foot in the water, interested, and wanting friendship.

Now he felt there was another thing going on. We were treating him as if he were a committed Christian. Something was missing. Something as simple as setting up chairs brought that to light. Was he ready to make a deeper commitment?

There was a struggle in his mind. There was a vast difference between looking like a Christian and being a converted believer. The First Christian Church in Brownsville, a small community church, was where his family worshipped every Sunday. Doug had a string of perfect attendance pins, and he would serve communion in the Sunday service. That was where his faith stopped. His personal life was anything but perfect. His life was a train wreck.

"I had this thought. *What have you done with your life?*" Doug explained to us when he realized he was a sinner.

"My life has been a disaster. I hurt many people; I messed up everything. Many nights I end up in bars, drinking and fighting because I am depressed. Then the thought came, '*Why not try God?*' So, I knelt beside my bed and surrendered my life to Jesus. Something amazing happened: peace washed over me, flowed over me, and I fell asleep with a smile on my face, content. So, I set up the chairs tonight. It was the first fruit of a changed heart."

CHAPTER 4

I WANT TO FOLLOW JESUS, BUT...

THE CAR ENGINE was still running. There was an awkward silence while I waited for Doug to speak. His words seemed to be stuck in his throat.

"Thanks for the ride home. It was a great Bible study tonight." I offered to help the conversation along. There was seriousness on his face, as well as pain and anger.

"Deb, I want to follow Jesus. I do, but..." There was another pause. I could tell that memories were flooding him, overwhelming him. "There is a man that I hate. I hate him so much that I dream of killing him. I dream about it so much that I have thought of ways to do that."

That was not the end of the evening that I was expecting. We both looked straight ahead; the car engine was still humming. How do I make this moment fit into my plans? I hoped for a relationship with him—the friendly guy who responded to the Gospel and joined our fellowship, who set up the chairs for our meetings now, and who talked about Jesus more than anything else? Thoughts of murder are disqualifying when you are thinking about a future husband.

"My life before coming to college was a disaster. Life for me stopped with a phone call from a girl I was dating. She told me she was pregnant. Against my parents' advice, no, against their demands, I got married. I have a son, Brian." If this conversation could get any worse,

I couldn't imagine. I understood the other side of Doug's life. There was so much pain. He had been hiding a secret dark life.

"Fred is my former wife's brother," he continued. "He harassed me, humiliated me, and mocked me. One day, I went to work in the morning. When I pulled up to my home at night, Fred was there. He was carrying the last piece of furniture out to a moving truck. They came as soon as I left for work and spent the day emptying my life. Everything I owned was gone. My son was gone."

Tears were welling up in his eyes and his voice cracked. "The police came and broke up the fight between us. It was a hopeless brawl for me. He's twice my size. For the next weeks, I stayed in that empty house, sleeping on the floor. Not a single thing was there—not a dish or a spoon. Nothing was left of my life."

He sat back in the seat, relaxing a bit. There was a sort of relief that came over him. This pain was so deep, and I was sure Jesus was the answer, but the questions and brokenness of his life were something I had not expected.

"Why did you stay there alone?" I wasn't sure if it was helpful to ask, but I was trying to bring some understanding and compassion to the moment.

"My father told me they would not welcome me to their home if I married her. My body broke out in boils from it all. I was drinking almost every night and getting into fights. My parents reconsidered and invited me home. Moving back into my old bedroom reinforced the fact that I had lost so much and it was the only place to lay my head."

I could remember him sharing in our Bible study about praying on his knees in this bedroom, the place where his grandmother had knelt before and prayed for him as a boy. His father had given him the book by Nicky Cruz, "Run Baby Run," and that story inspired him to go to college. He wanted to help people; therefore, he decided to become a social worker. I thought to myself, "He needs a social worker—not to become one."

That book is full of testimonies about Jesus and how He can change a life. It's amazing how God can work, even if Doug missed the Jesus parts. Something in that book gave him hope for his life.

"All of this happened before I met you and before I met Jesus. I caused all this pain, and I lost everything. I stopped seeing my son, even though there have been many court rulings in my favor since my divorce. Every time I go to see him, it is a battle. My son tells me he hates me. He is only four."

"Jesus will help you figure out your life, Doug. He can restore all the broken pieces. I am sure of it." With that, I gave him a reassuring hug, and as he drove away, I wondered about God's work in a person's life. I also wondered if my thoughts about a future with Doug were a little premature.

CHAPTER 5

CORRIE TEN BOOM

MY PRAYERS for Doug had a different focus now. "Lord, is he the one?" became "Lord, please help him forgive and find healing." I still had some hope for a future with him. But you can't hope to build a relationship when there is so much bitterness.

Our relationship changed after I heard his story. I was more cautious. He seemed less confident. I hoped something would happen that would change him. I could see that his shame and hatred for Fred were the backdrops for everything in his life, even his life as a follower of Jesus.

"Corrie Ten Boom is speaking at a Full Gospel meeting this weekend," I told him. "Do you want to go with me and hear her? She is a Dutch woman who had been in Ravensbruck, a concentration camp in World War II, and she has an amazing testimony. She wrote a book about it called *The Hiding Place*. He agreed to come, and I hoped that her message of forgiveness would help him.

The meeting hall at the Sheridan Hotel was jammed packed, with many people standing. After a song and some announcements, they introduced Corrie. She was frail-looking, with her signature gray bun of hair, and several ushers walked alongside her as she came to the podium. The room was quiet, with not a hint of whispers. She was a champion of the faith, a tramp for the Lord, a survivor of hell, and a bringer of hope.

"Fraulein, do you remember me?" She began sharing her story of meeting the guard who had murdered her sister in the concentration camp.

Corrie told of the darkness of that place of death and the light of Jesus that brought hope and salvation to the prisoners. I knew God had a message for Doug. Would he be able to hear it through the hatred in his own heart?

"I remember you," she said. This cruel guard was now asking for her forgiveness for an unforgivable and unthinkable act of violence that took her sister's life.

"Even as the anger and vengeful thoughts boiled through me, I saw the sin in them," she said. "Jesus Christ had died for this man."

"I prayed to Jesus, 'I cannot forgive him by myself; give me Your forgiveness.' From my shoulder, along my arm, and through my hand, a current seemed to pass from me to him, while into my heart sprang a love for this stranger that almost overwhelmed me. I discovered it is not on our forgiveness any more than our goodness that the world's healing hinges, but on His. When He tells us to love our enemies, He gives, along with the command, the love itself.

"So, I told him, 'Brother, I forgive you.' Thank You, Lord, for Romans 5:5. Thank You for bringing God's love into my heart through the Holy Spirit who was given to me. Thank You, Father, that Your love in me is stronger than my hatred and bitterness. At that moment, I knew I could forgive."

Many people in the room were crying. You could hear the quiet sobs even as she continued her message of forgiveness.

"Jesus will help you forgive if you can trust Him to help you. His love is stronger than your hatred and pain." Out of the corner of my view, I could see Doug, his eyes closed, his lips mouthing the prayer to forgive Fred, to forgive himself, and to trust Jesus.

We talked a little on the ride home. We both knew that was a turning point in Doug's life. Forgiveness is a key to unlocking the prisons of hatred and an open door to redemption and freedom. Jesus is the victor; He is indeed strong enough.

CHAPTER 6

TELL HIS STORY

"WE ARE GOING out to share our faith on campus tomorrow," Nick said. "See you there." When Doug hesitated, Nick followed up with a question. "You are coming, aren't you?"

There was a long silence, and Nick spoke with authority: "Doug, if you believe in Jesus, then you have a responsibility to share your faith with others. That is what Christians do. We tell His story."

The next day was awkward. Doug stumbled over his words and got dragged into arguments. When he was witnessing to a Buddhist student, he was almost convinced that there were many ways to God. It was essential to have Nick by his side, helping him to think through what had happened that day. That began his diligent search of the scriptures to add knowledge to his new faith. Every day, he would read the Bible for three or more hours. Soon he could hold his own in conversations, and his confidence grew.

That first day of witnessing was the last time Doug had to be nudged into sharing his faith. He had a fresh story to tell about how Jesus had changed his life. There was a deep passion in his heart that others needed to hear.

CHAPTER 7

STANTON HALL EVANGELISM

MY DORM ROOM was a center of activity. Girls stopping by to talk, ask questions, or just observe what was going on. Many believed in Jesus and attended Bible study at the Presbyterian Church.

From the beginning of our relationship, we shared this common passion for talking about Jesus. It was natural, compelling, and life-giving to see God use our lives to change the lives of other people.

CHAPTER 8

WALKING IN FREEDOM

GROWING UP, my home was filled with two distinct smells: cigarette smoke and beer. An open pack of Camels was always on our kitchen table, ashtrays in every room, and Iron City beer cans took up a shelf in the refrigerator. I am sure there was a lingering smell on my clothes when I headed off to school in the morning—the smell of a bar. I hated those smells. They intensified each night when my father found his way home from Chick's Bar down by the Monongahela River.

I hated that. I hated the atmosphere. Sometimes the things you hate become powerful temptations in your life. And so, it was for me when I arrived at Kitt Hall as a freshman. It didn't take long for the smell of smoke and alcohol to fill up my dorm room. Cigarette smoke was mixed with marijuana smoke.

I arrived on campus angry. I was mad that my father made me choose California for college. I was angry that I didn't have a choice. I was making new friends, and my new friends taught me to smoke. I was very sure that it was the worst use of fire that humanity had ever dreamed up. Thankfully, my desire to fit in and be cool was completely trumped by how sick I felt every time I breathed in the smoke from a cigarette.

I learned how to get past the taste and smell of alcohol. I would drown it out with cherry soda. And for a year, I found myself a social drinker, despite how wounded I had been by my father's abuse.

After my moment at Hair, when I surrendered to Jesus, I never felt convicted of drinking. I judged my own life and compared it to the lives of others. I thought I was in control of this and not as bad as my father. My room was the Jesus hangout.

That ended one afternoon as I was sitting in my dorm room talking to a friend about Jesus.

"Deb, are you drinking?" She questioned me and was upset.

"Well, I have a drink here, but I am not drunk."

"I don't understand. Isn't that something that destroys people's lives? Why would you continue to drink if your choices could hurt other people and give them a license to harm themselves? I thought Christians had a higher standard than that. I am not interested in hearing any more about your God if you aren't interested in changing how you live."

And that was it: a very closed door, a lost opportunity. I could have defended my choice to have a social drink with a very self-righteous defense. After all, Jesus turned water into wine at a wedding.

But the impact of her calling me out changed my perspective. What I gained from social drinking compared to what I lost with the closed door made it unreasonable for me. There was no comparison. It was a small thing to let go of, and I never missed it. I believe that was God's protection over my life and my family. My father's alcoholism could have become mine in hard times if I had had that to turn to when I wanted to numb my pain when faced with hard times in life.

I also know that it was His protection of my family. Many committed Christians who drink regret it. The choices they make to drink in moderation become excesses in their children's lives. So, freedom for me in this area was about letting go of an unnecessary and potentially harmful social choice, removing hindrances from my testimony, and the negative influences I might have on others who might stumble because of my choices.

In America, 85 percent of adults have drunk alcohol in their lives, and most do it in moderation, but 25 percent of adults engage in some binge drinking each month.

Most of our friends drink casually, but being sensitive to the influence my example has on others, I cannot join them.

But food does not bring us closer to God: We are no worse if we do not eat, and no better if we do.

> Be careful, however, that your freedom does not become a stumbling block to the weak. For if someone with a weak conscience sees you who are well informed eating in an idol's temple, will he not be encouraged to eat food sacrificed to idols? Therefore, if what I eat causes my brother to stumble, I will never eat meat again, so that I will not cause him to stumble.
> 1 Corinthians 8:8–10,13 BSB

I never missed drinking even one glass. And I was always grateful for my decision.

Doug had a struggle with alcohol. It was both his go-to escape from pain and his social connection with friends at the bar. Many fights happened in situations where he had been drinking. Many poor decisions almost destroyed his life. Yet he never thought that his newfound faith in Jesus should change his long-developed habit of consuming alcohol. He was an evangelist from the beginning and would invite his friends to our college Bible study, and afterward, everyone would follow him to the bar for drinks and a conversation about God. It was just what was normal for him.

Then one night, he was sitting at the bar with a beer in his hand, and the thought came to his mind. "I do not need this anymore. I don't need this to feel accepted. I don't need this for fun. I don't need this when I am mad. I don't need this when I am upset. I have found a new life. This old way of coping and belonging will no longer be a part of it."

He pushed the beer away, and that part of his life was over. Walking away from the powerful bondage was his freedom, and Jesus met the deepest part of his needs.

When I had my DNA analyzed, I found my biological grandfather. I had never met him; I never even knew his name. My father had no relationship with him, yet his life of alcohol abuse mirrored his father's. The family members I found through the Ancestry match all described him as a drunk who was addicted to alcohol. I realized that there was a hereditary tendency for addiction. It marked most of my father's life, and even though he was free after his commitment to Christ, he died prematurely because of it.

CHAPTER 9

EXPLO '72

SMALL GROUPS like the one meeting at the Millers' house were popping up everywhere.

California Fellowship, our Intervarsity group, met each Thursday evening. Our group was growing each week as more students became Christians.

While the country was going through a cultural upheaval with social norms changing, political unrest, and the Vietnam War raging, there was another upheaval. This was a move of God that Christians had prayed and longed for.

We heard stories of people being filled with the Holy Spirit in churches scattered across the United States: Calvary Chapel in California and the Catholic Charismatic Renewal in Pittsburgh. People were encountering God. The artists were awakening, and Christian music had its beginnings with Love Song and Amy Grant. Bill Bright from Campus Crusade and Billy Graham were at the forefront, bringing leadership. Pat Robertson also began his TV network.

Cathy Geda brought a brochure to our group in the early spring of 1972. "Something is happening in Dallas this summer, everyone," she said. "Christians from across the country are going to come together for this big event called Explo '72 from June 12–17. We should all go."

We never even prayed about it. God was calling His revived church to gather in Dallas, and we had to be a part of it. Within a few days, we had saved our spots on a bus leaving from California, PA, and decided how to raise the funds. We had a Jesus Walk through the community and ask people to sponsor our group to go. We visited businesses and asked churches and friends for support. All of us signed up. What would it be like to see 100,000 Christians at the Cotton Bowl? It was going to be amazing.

Our budget provided for us to stay in tents in Tent City. We were going to have two tents: a guys' tent and a girls' tent. The first morning, as they dropped us off at the stadium, it was astounding. A sea of people gathered in His name. You could hear people singing everywhere—hippies and traditional older folks alike. There was a special time of outreach in the afternoons, going door to door and sharing the Gospel. Bill Bright, Billy Graham and Andraé Crouch headlined the program.

Our view of the church had changed. Just weeks before we thought we were the only true believers in our little California fellowship. Now, we could see a glimpse of the kingdom of God: old and young, traditional and radical Jesus people. For the first time, we experienced outreach on a huge scale. The Four Spiritual Laws tract was an effective tool used to present the Gospel.

A storm came on the third night and knocked most of the tents down. I had warned Doug to stay away from the Holy Spirit-type people. I was primarily raised in the Presbyterian Church and wasn't ready to see my new boyfriend sucked into a crazy Pentecostal group. "Just walk away from anyone talking about speaking in tongues," I told him. "That is a sure sign they are on the fringe."

After the storm came through, people helped each other, and made new friends. I saw Doug talking with a group that I was concerned about. Dennis Gary was with him. About 3:00 A.M., I could hear Doug praying and shouting, and it wasn't English.

I raced out, and there they were. Dennis and Doug were laying on the muddy ground, praying, and not even aware that I was standing over them.

"Doug, stop this!" I yelled. "This is not from the Lord."

He never acknowledged me, my words, or the many others who were trying to sleep nearby and were shouting for them to be quiet.

He later told me they prayed for Dennis, and the power of God hit him and he fell over. I didn't believe that story for a minute.

"I prayed, 'God, what you did for him, do that for me,'" Doug said, "and the next minute I was on the ground praying."

I didn't believe that either! What was worse, this was a guy I wanted to marry. I wasn't looking for someone who was into the charismatic experience.

CHAPTER 10

MINI EXPO

THE EXPERIENCE at Explo '72 sparked an idea in Doug's mind. He could envision that experience happening on our college campus in the spring of '73. He didn't see his limits, or that we had zero experience organizing an event like that. But our small band of Jesus People at the Christian Fellowship were all in, filled with faith from our trip to Dallas.

So, we invited Pat Boone. We began the negotiations and planning, and we were filled with expectations. Our faith was flying high until we received the contract from Pat's people, and $5,000 was the price tag for having an evening with Pat.

We didn't count the cost before building. When we realized our bank account of $200 was not sufficient for this commitment, we experienced our first crisis of faith.

Didn't we pray about this? Didn't God provide for our trip to Dallas? Why didn't we have enough money for this? And most of all, how could a Christian hero expect a handful of college students to come up with that amount of money?

We were disappointed. Our group had talked about it so much, proclaiming our faith that it would happen, but a huge public embarrassment was now part of our reputation.

We lost our dream for the event, but we still had a scheduled date for our event: April 15. Sitting with our discouraged team, trying to find the faith to keep going, one student spoke up: "I have heard about an excellent speaker, Loren Cunningham. He lives in Switzerland. He leads a missions organization called Youth With A Mission (YWAM). Are you okay with me writing an invitation letter?"

We were back on track with our dream of hosting an event on our campus. Our team sent a letter to Loren Cunningham, an unknown speaker who would change everything in our lives. Loren replied to our letter and said he had only one open date for speaking available, and it was our date. He prayed and felt it was right to come. There were no demands for money or special accommodations.

We needed music. After several failed attempts to find a local Christian band, someone suggested that we contact a guy from Ohio. They heard he was an excellent guitarist. He traveled with a friend, and he would come for just gas money. So, we contacted Phil Keaggy, and he brought Peter York along.

Our plans for Pat Boone failed; God's plans for Loren Cunningham and Phil Keaggy succeeded.

Loren stayed with Doug's parents, and it honored them to have a special guest in their home, though we still didn't know who Loren was or how that one night would change our lives. We gave Loren $100, and he graciously received it with, "Thank you. This will get me to my next stop."

Phil was grateful for the gas money to get back to Ohio. Right around the corner, Phil became one of the most famous musicians of the Jesus People movement, and from his gracious and humble beginnings, he made a tremendous impact on our campus.

Hundreds of students showed up for the meeting. Loren spoke about apologetics. "You say there are no absolutes. Can you be absolutely sure about that?" Phil and Peter brought their fresh sound and powerful lyrics to our ears, and hundreds responded to an invitation to follow Jesus. Doug's friend, Ken Barnes, was one of them.

We experienced a campus revival that almost didn't happen because of our inexperience and presumption. God turned our roadblocks around and brought His plan, which would mark our lives for the next four decades.

That experience changed us. We knew God could give us second chances, and we had an even greater vision for what might happen through us and the impact we could have on our community.

CHAPTER 11

AMEN CORNER

DOUG HAD many moments where sharing Christ brought conflict in the classroom. He was a social work major, and it was the 1970s. Many of our professors were atheists with an agenda to stamp out faith when they saw it in their students.

"Let's begin this class with the presupposition that there is no God, shall we?"

That is a powerful statement when it is expressed by a teacher who has the authority to pass or fail you in a class. Everyone else in the class nodded in submission with little sign that they were relinquishing their faith without even a small protest in their body language.

However, Doug put up his hand and waved it to get the professor's attention. "Well, sir, I believe in God, and I would not agree. I can't go along with that to start this class." There was stunned silence from the class as they awaited the professor's response. Dr. Jack was surprised. Maybe this was the first time that his opening statement had been challenged. He just ignored Doug's comment and began his lecture.

A few minutes into it, there were other provocative comments thrown out as truth. In the room's corner, there was a hand waving high in the air.

"Sir, I am wondering how you came to that conclusion," Doug challenged. "That is not what I believe or what I have seen to be true in people's lives."

"Thank you for your comment. Let's move on."

Before the class ended, Dr. Jack responded again to his waving hand with a sigh. He was clearly upset at the ongoing disruption in the class.

"Okay, what would you like to say from the Amen Corner?"

That was Doug's identity in the class. His new faith was genuine and affected every area of his life. He would not get run over by challenges from friends or professors. He didn't have answers for every challenge, but he knew when something didn't line up with the foundations that were being built in his life. When there was an honest challenge to his faith he could not answer, he went to the Bible and to Christian friends to ask for help.

He learned to defend his faith, and he stood for the truth, even if he was the only voice of reason. Many times, other students would tell him how they were afraid to stand up in class. They were believers and had been encouraged by his faith. Other students would ask how he knew the answers, and many of them came to follow Jesus and became part of our campus fellowship.

Dr. Jack had a profound impact on Doug's life. At the end of this semester, he asked Doug to come for a meeting with the other social work department professors. "Doug, we realize you are one very focused young man. You are passionate to make a difference in this world. However, you are going to have a tough time trying to fit that passion into the field of social work. We suggest you turn your focus and become a preacher."

That was unsolicited yet expert advice. Doug saw God was leading him to his calling to bring the Gospel to others.

When your faith is genuine, and you are living it out in your daily life, your honesty and sincerity affect others. Your faith is contagious.

Some say that people do not want to hear about God and that people want to be left alone when it comes to God. Forty years of living with boldness have taught us that those are myths. They simply aren't true. We have found yearning hearts in every country, in every age group, and in every social group. People are often not interested in clichés or hearing worn-out rhetoric.

Our message needs to be clear, compelling, and from the heart. From his Amen Corner days until now, Doug has brought God's truth, and people have responded.

CHAPTER 12

JESUS FREAK

"LORD, SO many of the girls in my dorm are becoming Christians. Why doesn't Janet even make eye contact with me? What is the problem with her?" Being an RA (Resident Assistant) in Stanton Hall, a girls' dorm on the California State College campus, was a great job. I always had someone to chat with, and now that I was living for the Lord, those conversations were often about Jesus.

Janet was also an RA, and we had dorm meetings together. She never spoke to me unless it was necessary. She made a point of disappearing from any potential situation where we might have to interact with each other. I just didn't understand what her problem was. Wasn't I a nice person?

The Lord answered my prayer with, "The problem is with you. She's reacting to your pride."

I wasn't prideful. Was I? I assumed it had nothing to do with me. And maybe there were reasons she was avoiding me that had to do with some problems in her life. Yet, something I was portraying to her was making it more difficult for her to see that God was seeking her.

If I was in her way, how could I get out of it? My first thought was to return her snub. Or I could just ignore her. That didn't seem like the best approach. I knew what I had to do.

Our rooms were on the same floor, and I made my way down the hall to her door. I was rehearsing my apology in my mind along the way. "I am sorry you were offended...No, I am sorry you have a problem with me." That was still about her having a problem. I was sweating, and my heart was racing.

Knock. Knock. "Hi there. I just wanted to talk to you for a few minutes." I didn't wait to be invited in. I just stepped past her and spun around. "I can tell I have been offending you, and I am sorry. I didn't realize. Please forgive me."

I don't know how I expected her to react, but before I could get the next words out of my mouth, I was standing in her room by myself with the door slammed shut. She mumbled something under her breath, sounding like, "Jesus freak!"

That clearly wasn't helpful.

In the next few days, my prayers for Janet were more about my heart and asking the Lord to help me continue to be kind but also humble and give her space.

Knock. Knock. This time, it was my door. I opened it to find Janet standing there with tears streaming down her face. "I need Jesus. Please pray for me."

She shared with me some of her heartbreak stories and how she was reacting to me. She was sometimes hostile to me because of things in her own heart. We became fast friends. July 2, 1972, was the day that everything changed in Janet's life, and Psalm 147:3 became her verse. It says, "He heals the brokenhearted and binds up their wounds."

On February 2, 1974, Janet was a bridesmaid at our wedding. That summer, she went to Brazil with us on our first mission trip. She later lived with us in the extra apartment in our basement and taught at Chapel Christian School, which I helped start. Janet later became a Wycliffe Bible Translator in Sabah (North Borneo) in East Malaysia. I thought about how that "I am sorry" moment opened the door to an amazing friendship and how her life has affected so many.

CHAPTER 13

FEBRUARY 2

I STOOD in the foyer of the Presbyterian Church of California. It was our wedding day. The church was filled with family and friends, ready to share in this joyful time. My father stood beside me, shaking, and his face was ashen. The music stopped, and I could hear footsteps as Doug and his groomsmen walked to the front of the beautiful church.

To everyone's surprise, Doug went straight up to the pulpit. "Welcome, friends and family. Thank you for coming. As I get married today, I want to take this time to tell you what has happened over the past two years. I want you to know what God has done. Many of you know I have made many mistakes in my life. Two years ago, I was walking on this campus when a stranger approached me. He told me about Jesus and invited me to a campus fellowship group that met upstairs in this very church."

Everyone sat quietly, surprised and wondering what he would say next.

"I was very lost and looking for the answers to life. Whether out of boredom, curiosity or because this student showed me some kindness, I took a step and showed up at the meeting. I had attended church all my life and had perfect attendance pins to show for it. And at the same time, I had a very broken life; I was hurt, and I hurt many people. Though I would say I was a Christian, my life in no way showed that I was a follower of Jesus. That day began a new life for me."

He took a moment to pause, looking around the sanctuary. "Several weeks later, I was walking through my house, and a question rang in my heart: 'What have you done with your life?' I had caused many people pain.

"Another question came, 'What do you want from your life?'

"My answer was that I wanted to be successful and have money, but I had made such a mess of my life and hurt so many people.

"Again, I heard, '*Why not trust me with your life?*' And at that moment, I saw my life in such a different way. I saw my need for forgiveness. I knew God was reaching out to me. I went to my bedroom, knelt beside my bed, and surrendered my life to Jesus. This was the place where I often saw my grandmother praying, and I think mostly for me.

"As I went to sleep that night, I felt peace. This was the starting point of a new life. A short time later, my mom said to me, 'It seems like another person is living in your body. You are smiling again.'

"These last two years have been life-changing for me. Now, as I begin my life with Deb, I have a different focus, a different heart, and a different future. I want to invite you to think about your life and trust Jesus as your Savior and Lord, too."

Our wedding bulletin included the small tract, Steps to Peace with God. Doug led them in quiet prayer. I don't know if anyone prayed with him, but I know we began our marriage with a testimony of God's grace that would carry us throughout the rest of our lives.

February 2 was also Groundhog Day. Because of the Arab oil embargo and gas lines, we faced the uncertainty of getting gas. As we pulled away for our honeymoon in my '67 Mustang, we had a tank of gas and needed God's provision on day one.

Gas was being rationed, and gas stations were required to close on Sundays. We wondered where we would find gas the next day. We began our marriage with a prayer for God's miraculous provision.

The next morning, we were driving through the Laurel mountains and looking for a place to eat. We prayed and expected God's provision. Right ahead, there was an open gas station. No one else was there. The attendant filled our car, and we drove away, amazed. A short time later, we returned to find the station closed. I opened it just for us.

PART TWO

Alliance Chapel

Elizabeth and Belle Vernon, Pennsylvania

CHAPTER 14

A NEW OPPORTUNITY

I ENJOYED teaching kindergarten at Library Christian School. My life turned out differently from my freshman plans upon entering college. My major was social work, to begin with. After Jesus changed my heart, I recognized that teaching was what I loved and was called to do.

When I graduated, I wanted to teach. But where? Unbeknownst to me, my father had spoken with a few friends in our school district. I was looking for a Christian school. I realized that the freedom to share the Gospel as I taught was essential to me.

Unexpectedly, I got a phone call when I was praying about what job to take.

"Is this Debra Roberts?"

"Yes," I answered.

"Congratulations! We have hired you to teach first grade, so make sure you apply before our next school board meeting." They offered me a job that I didn't apply for and didn't want.

"Well, sir," I replied. "I am not sure about this."

"Are you crazy? This is an amazing opportunity. It is all arranged. I am sure we will have a greater salary than your other offer."

That was more than true. It was six times more than the one at the Baptist Library. This was one time I had to choose to follow Jesus, regardless of the financial consequences.

Teaching kindergarten at the Library Baptist Academy was a good fit for me. I loved the parents and the children, and I came alive in the classroom.

CHAPTER 15

JESUS IS LORD

"I HAD AN IDEA while driving home through Brownsville tonight."

This was one of the thousand ideas that Doug shared with me. He dreamed about new things. Brownsville was a small town on the Monongahela River. It was the place where the Tunney family settled. In the past, it was a coal-mining town. The downtown area was becoming like a ghost town, with many empty, boarded-up stores.

I leaned forward to listen to his idea.

"You know that bar in the middle of town?" He asked. "The one next to the parking lot. I was thinking we could paint a message across that massive red brick wall so that as people drive by, they could see it."

He had the idea; I had the practical thoughts of how that would happen.

By the following weekend, Doug had recruited friends to help, had the paint donated, made a template, and had the bar owner agree to the plan. We painted "Jesus Is Lord" in ten-foot-high white letters, proclaiming to our town that Jesus was happening there.

CHAPTER 16

BRAZIL AIRLIFT '74

"DOUG, WILL you come with us this summer to Brazil?" Brother Earl invited us to join the Jesus Airlift '74 outreach in July.

We were at Christ's Castle in Franklin, Pennsylvania, for a retreat with Earl Tygert. He was our mentor and inspired us to love God's Word. He officiated at our marriage ceremony.

"Earl, thanks for the invitation," Doug replied. "I will pray about it!"

Doug's response received a look of displeasure. There was an awkward pause.

"Well, now, isn't that spiritual?" Earl teased us with a smile.

I glanced at Doug.

"Well, isn't this how you are supposed to respond when someone asks this kind of question?" Doug asked him.

Earl answered that question with a "NO." "That is what people say when they have zero intention of doing something," Earl said. "It's the cop-out answer, the passive avoidance answer, and almost no one really prays about it. They just move on."

We had been married for just a few months and were expecting a baby in December. Praying about it seemed like the right answer.

"Please pray about it," Earl replied, "but why don't you pray like this: 'Lord, I have a chance to go to Brazil. If you don't want me to go, please let me know. Otherwise, I am going?"

With that, we said our goodbyes and headed home from Christ's Castle. It had been an inspiring weekend with the students from our California Fellowship. We had a new way of praying. We were going unless the Lord said no.

When you flip the focus of your prayer in this way, it is more serious. We prayed for the next few weeks, asking God if we should go. Each time, we felt peace in our hearts. It was a growing sense of peace and confidence. Brother Earl was happy when we called to sign up for the mission trip.

The next few months were filled with preparations: birth certificates, passports, and shots!

I mentioned our plans at my next prenatal doctor's appointment and asked what shots I needed. The room got icy quiet.

"You are planning to go *where* this summer?"

"Brazil, for four weeks!" I smiled, hoping to lighten the mood that Dr. Cabrera had set.

"You need a yellow fever shot, but pregnant women cannot take this shot." He sighed and continued, "Instead, you would need a signed waiver from your doctor—me! I am from South America, and I know the potential dangers there. I will not give you a waiver. This is too dangerous. You could get very sick. You could lose your baby. I will not be a part of this risky venture. You must cancel your plans."

With that, he left the room. He closed the door louder than usual as an exclamation point to his nonnegotiable response to my question.

Okay, that was a closed-door answer to a prayer if I ever heard one. The doctor said there was no way.

We prayed that night, "Lord, the doctor says no."

Yet we deeply sensed that we were to continue our plans. We were just newlyweds. We didn't have a long history of being united in prayers like that, but both of us were convinced that we were to go.

We raised the funds for our trip. We saved money from each of our paychecks. Friends stepped up and gave us gifts to help us. We even got a check in the mail from Pittsburgh Steel. They had made a mistake in Doug's pay a few years before, and the audit was in his favor. We did everything possible, yet we were thousands short of the trip's cost.

"Lord, our finances seem to say no." We prayed again.

At that moment, Doug had a picture come into his mind: his '47 Plymouth Coupe, his dream antique car. He didn't say a word for a few minutes, and then, "Lord, I am willing, but I love my car. If there is another plan, please let me know."

His treasured car, a bit of an idol for him, sold in a week, and the price covered the rest of our trip. We had the money, but we still didn't have the doctor's release. So, we sent the funds to Life Ministries to reserve our spots.

The months passed, and I had several more doctor visits. Each time I brought up the trip, Dr. Cabrera had a sterner way of saying, "No way."

This could be a classic case of being stuck between a rock and a hard place. God was saying "yes." The doctor was saying, "no." What does faith look like for a twenty-two-year-old girl learning to hear God's voice? I trusted the Lord would take care of the baby I was carrying and me.

Our bags were packed the day before our trip, our passports were ready, and tickets were purchased. I took one more step and called the Brownsville clinic. It was one last chance, hoping the doctor would change his mind. We had no plan B, but plan A seemed like a shot in the dark.

"Hello, this is Dr. Cabrera's office. No, the doctor is out this week. Can I help you? Yes, I can sign a pregnancy waiver for a deferment for your shot. I will be in tomorrow morning at nine."

I put the phone down on the receiver. Our plane was supposed to leave at twelve. There was just enough time to get the signed paper and drive to the airport. The nurse handed me the waiver with a smile in the morning. When I got in the car, I was both excited and terrified. I felt like I had just stolen something. I felt like I had just passed a test. In a few hours, I was 30,000 feet in the air. It was my first flight and my first radical leap of faith. I was walking on uncharted waters. The next four weeks would change my life forever.

Brazil greeted us with warm sunshine and even warmer friends. When we met our translators, it was a quick friendship. Brazil was an open mission field. Each city we visited represented a new door for the Gospel.

We began our day in God's Word, reading through the book of Romans, a chapter each day, and eating breakfast. Earl's famous line was "no Bible, no breakfast." Then a team meeting, prayer, teaching from Romans, lunch, and then to the streets.

This outreach was so new to us. Our Brazilian bus driver drove us to parks. One team member would play a worship song. Our team would sing, and a crowd would gather around us.

"We are friends from America, and we have come to share with you that Jesus loves you." The Portuguese translation followed.

Every day, hundreds of individuals responded to the Gospel. For each outreach, we left a team behind to pray and back us up. Halfway into the trip, several team members came down with a fever. They were very sick and stayed back at the school where we were housed. I became concerned. No one besides Doug knew about my doctor's warning. During the next few days, more of the team became seriously ill and stayed back, and none recovered quickly.

On the way to our host pastor's house, I felt hot. I thought it was my imagination, with all the others getting sick. I felt hotter and dizzier. By the time we arrived, I had to be helped out of the bus and into the pastor's house. They provided a quiet room for me to lie down. That night, I stayed back from the outreach and rested at the school.

My head was spinning with the heat of my body and with the guilt of putting myself in this situation. I could remember Dr. Cabrera saying, "You could get very sick. You could lose your baby."

In my desperation, I prayed for myself. I put both hands on my head and cried, "Lord, you know everything. Please heal me. Keep my baby safe!"

My head was just as hot as before.

"Lord, I am trusting in you alone. Please heal me and keep my baby safe." I felt my head. It seemed hotter than before.

"Lord, please."

I could feel the change: a cold sweat and stronger breathing. Strength was pouring into me. As I washed the sweat away with a cool cloth, I felt renewed. The rest of the team was sick for many days, some as long as a week. I knew my recovery resulted from God's touch and healing power.

When we returned to the States, over 700 people had prayed to receive Jesus. I tasted what it meant to be a missionary. Something inside me resounded with the idea that this first trip was the first fruits of a life called to the nations.

CHAPTER 17

MATTHEW 11

OUR TRIP to Brazil was our first step into missions. We gained a new heart for people from other nations who had never heard of Jesus. We became more aware of those family members at home who had heard but never understood the Gospel.

On our flight home, Doug told Earl Tygert, "It seems so easy to tell strangers about Jesus. Now when we go home, I think about my family. My parents attend church weekly, and I had perfect attendance pins myself, but I never heard the Gospel."

Earl shared a scripture from Matthew 11:1. After Jesus had instructed his disciples and sent them out to share the Good News in Chapter 10, He did something very interesting. He went to teach and preach in Galilee, in their city, to their people and their families. The Greek translation says, "In their towns." He knew the sacrifice they were making to follow Him, and He also cared about the people that were closest to their hearts.

"Doug, you can trust God with your family," Earl encouraged him.

We were excited to tell stories about our trip when we returned. The gifts we brought back helped us to share about our new friends from a faraway land and to help our loved ones get a glimpse into our hearts to bring the Gospel.

Doug's first attempt to reach out to the Tunney clan the previous Christmas fell flat. The Christmas pie gift exchange allowed him to bring some "witness" to his family by giving Bibles to family members. These gifts were received with a less-than-warm reaction, and he heard several people joke about not wanting him to get their names next year. They also called him Billy Graham when they thought he wasn't listening, but he heard the whispers, which was discouraging.

We decided to be a little more low-key, pray, and act naturally about our faith. There were open doors to share when we looked for them. We prayed more than we shared and trusted the Lord to make opportunities.

After our Mini Explo, Doug was inspired to continue creating events that would benefit people in our community. We heard of an opportunity to bring a special speaker to Doug's high school. Rock Royer was a well-known football coach for the Navy, and now he coaches for Liberty University. He was also an outspoken Christian known as "Coach Born Again."

When Doug visited the principal to ask if he could use the school auditorium for the meeting, the principal was shocked. "Doug, never in my wildest dreams did I think you would be a Christian and that you would ask to set up a meeting like this. I am happy to help."

That was the perfect opportunity to invite his family. There was going to be a special speaker at the hometown school. Doug's mom was the only one who accepted the invitation to come. When Rock gave his testimony, she was focused and listened to every word. "If you would like to make a commitment to follow Jesus, please come forward, and we will pray for you," he said at the end of his message.

Connie Tunney was the first one out of her seat to walk to the front of the gym.

The next summer, at the Tunney family reunion, Doug's uncle, Ernie, pulled him aside and told him he had become a believer. A

Christian had knocked on his door and shared the Gospel with him. Matthew 11 was becoming real in our family. It repeatedly happened throughout the next few years until the reunions became more of a gathering of Christians. We were not the ones to reach out to most of them, but Jesus was the One who went to our city when we did His bidding in our lives.

CHAPTER 18

TRUE REVIVAL AT THE CHAPEL

"DO NOT BE amazed that I said to you, 'You must be born again.' The wind blows where it wishes and you hear the sound of it, but do not know where it comes from and where it is going; so is everyone who is born of the Spirit." Nicodemus said to Him, "How can these things be?"
John 3:7–9 BSB

REVIVAL. People pray for it; I have seen marquee signs on church buildings announcing meetings that promise it. Yet it is like the wind. Ecclesiastes 11:5 BSB says, *"As you do not know the path of the wind, or how the body is formed in a mother's womb, so you cannot understand the work of God, the Maker of all things."*

I am sure that I have experienced a supernatural move of God several times in my life. I recognized it, was amazed by it, and was so thankful to have experienced it.

In the late fall of 1973, Gail Koslosky, a friend of my mother, told us about The Chapel. It was a CMA church in Elizabeth. On our first visit, we arrived early. The parking lot was already overfilled, and cars were lined up along Simpson Howell Road.

We were thankful to find one of the few remaining seats. The service went on for hours, but we hardly noticed. Preacher Bill spoke, and we liked him right away. He was young and inspiring. The church was full of families and young adults. After the service, there was an unscheduled time of fellowship. People just didn't want to go home. There was something so wonderful about God's presence.

The Chapel felt like home. It was like Eden had come for us. Each service gave us a fresh understanding of the Bible. New people were added to the church daily as friends brought their friends to meet Jesus. "Just like in the book of Acts," I often thought to myself.

After our wedding and Brazil mission trip in 1994, Preacher Bill asked us to join a team of three couples that would provide leadership for a new young adult group. They named themselves "Power Group."

Our first meeting with them was discouraging. Love Song, a Christian band, played in Pittsburgh and all the young adults attended the concert. Members of the leaders' group were the only ones in attendance. This happened many of the nights over the next few weeks. A core group soon developed, and we could count on them every Friday night. They brought their friends to church and then on Friday nights. Doug fasted every Friday and shared a word with the group. He chose a different topic every week, but it seemed the message always ended up having "Falling in love with Jesus" as the theme.

In the early church, the Lord added to their number daily. So, it was with Power Group. We didn't need to preach about bringing friends to church. The young people had found reality in Christ. They wanted their friends to be in on the wonderful discovery. We began a second discipleship meeting in our home on Tuesday nights.

CHAPTER 19

INNOCENCE AND MINISTRY MELTDOWN

THE CHAPEL was amazing. Preacher Bill was full of faith, and each message was filled with something fresh that God was teaching him. Rich was the head elder. He was a business owner, a church builder, and a pilot who owned a flight school. Rich had a vision to reach across denominational barriers and bring people together. He was one of the founders of the Jesus Gatherings.

It was perfect. God was moving. It was a revival.

We outgrew our church building. Each service was packed. Cars filled the parking lot and overflowed down the main road. Every chair in the sanctuary was filled, and the foyer was filled. More chairs were placed on the stage, leaving only a space for Preacher Bill to stand at the podium to speak. No one wanted to leave at the end of any service. Afterward, the Power Group would all go to a restaurant to continue to fellowship and talk about Jesus to anyone who would listen.

I thought this must be how it felt in the days after Pentecost. The church was in one accord. People were coming to faith. Lives were being changed. We were living right in the middle of a mighty move of God.

We had an innocence about us; we were trusting and vulnerable. In that environment, it was easy to surrender to God's plans for our lives because we knew we were made for heaven and were tasting it here on earth.

The leaders planned for a new church building. Rich was the perfect leader to have with his construction experience. Preacher Bill was the perfect pastor to inspire the congregation to embrace a new challenge and give so the church could expand. We all knew that we needed more room so more people could experience God's presence and become followers of Jesus.

Then something unexpected and unbelievable happened.

"Can you have dinner with us? We would love to spend some time with you." Rich and Alice invited us for an evening of fellowship. We enjoyed the great food they prepared and shared the evening with them. And then it happened—something unexpected and unwelcome.

"Doug, Deb, you are doing such a great job with our young people," they encouraged us. We smiled, receiving the compliment. "And you know our church needs to grow to accommodate all the new people."

We nodded yes.

"And Preacher Bill... Well, he just isn't hearing from God about this new direction. In fact, we have realized that we can't trust him to lead our church right now."

We were stunned. We just stared without responding. There was trouble in paradise; somehow, we were being drawn into the middle of a political power struggle.

Several days later, we received another seemingly innocent invitation for a meal with Preacher Bill and his family. And it was a carbon copy of the previous meeting with Rich and Alice. "Great job with the Power Group, Doug. We look forward to what God has for us and are so glad you are a part of our team. But we have a concern. Rich, well, he seems to be on another path. He is a rebel, you know. Business owners are like that, and they just want power. I realize we can't trust him to make this decision."

The leaders we loved were showing signs of weakness that we never expected—jealousy, competition, gossip and manipulation. This schism spread. The rest of the elders took sides, choosing between Rich and Bill. Part of the congregation left with Rich to build a new church on a property nearby. Preacher Bill and the other elders took the other group to a new property in Belle Vernon and established the Christian Center.

We went with our pastor, but we went with a broken heart. As much as we tried to let it go and move on, resentment was building in my heart. It wasn't for what had been done to us. But it was for the harm that was done to the Church. A split church has so much fallout: disillusioned and angry people are all pointing to the other side over a perceived injustice. The judgments and accusations were not anything we had ever expected. We just chose not to talk about it.

CHAPTER 20

FALLEN HERO

PREACHER BILL was our hero. When we joined the staff as youth pastors, and it seemed like heaven to us.

After the move to Belle Vernon, many changes happened. There was a big change for the congregation to be in a new building at a new location.

We noticed Preacher Bill seemed more distant. His preaching was full of leftovers from the past. The exciting revival seemed to stall. The elders called for a time of prayer and fasting for the church.

Toward the end of that dedicated prayer time, Doug came to me with a very concerned look. "I just saw Preacher Bill out in the parking lot, and it was so strange," he said. "He was hiding between the cars."

It was only a few days later that we got the call. Bill had run away with another woman and left his family. We could not believe our pastor and friend had fallen away from the Lord.

I remember those days; all the weight of Bill's failings was laid on our very young shoulders. Our phones rang with upset church members asking questions. They were discouraged, angry, and wanted answers. We had none.

Our friend and hero had done the unimaginable. We were disappointed and disillusioned. It was a public disaster. The reputation of the church and of the move of God was up for ridicule. I can remember feeling so angry, and then the phone call came to shock us all. It was Bill, asking to talk with Doug. He confessed he was wrong and wanted to come home.

Bill was restored to his family and tried to return to lead the church, but the elders, in their wisdom, refused. He then started another church down the road, which had little of the original glory and impact. God's mercy was poured into his life. There was redemption and forgiveness. His life was restored, yet there were consequences that followed him. He eventually moved away and worked for a secular job, but he kept his family together.

Before this, we had a very naïve trust in leaders. Of course, the Bible is full of extraordinary leaders, some of whom had very devastating falls. We somehow felt that revival took us beyond that, and I think Bill felt invincible. He later told us he had unwisely opened himself up to temptation by spending time with women in ministry without accountability. Often, several other women approached him. He resisted them until this thought came to him: you deserve more than you have in your marriage. That was the seed that grew into a choice that shipwrecked his life and derailed the revival.

Our church survived because of God's help. Our very dedicated leaders led us through. Sin was exposed, forgiveness was extended, and the church endured.

We had a choice when faced with the fall of our friend and mentor. First, we forgave. Then, we kept our eyes on the Lord and not on the man. Until that time, we had loyalty to leadership without limits. After this time, we had 100 percent loyalty to God and a cautious loyalty to leaders. We realized men will fail. If we saw something like that again we would confront it.

We have seen churches where the failings and sins of the leaders were covered over to protect the reputation of the church. The result was always worse.

We also knew we had to protect our own lives. As leaders, we would be a target of the enemy. Doug and I made a very serious commitment in our marriage to never put ourselves in vulnerable places. We protected ourselves. We went out of our way to be accountable to each other. One man's sin caused so many negative ripples. So, we wanted our lives to produce life.

CHAPTER 21

MAGIC LANTERN

OUR FRIENDS, Denny and Donna Moor, lived in the small town of Smithton. When our church moved to Belle Vernon, they became very involved in helping us lead the Power Group young adult ministry. When we visited them, we drove by the Magic Lantern, an X-rated movie house.

Growing up, Doug had a closet full of adult magazines and embraced the playboy mentality. The results hurt him as a young man, but God freed him from its power early in his walk with Him. If we entered a store that displayed suggestive magazines, he would always walk away from the display. We committed to not watching R-rated movies and asked the Lord to protect our hearts from the distorted influences that seemed to be everywhere.

Before we left for YWAM in 1979, we spent the summer with a team in an outreach house in Smithton. In our times of prayer, God put it on our hearts to pray for those caught up in the power of pornography at the Magic Lantern. For weeks, we did standing protests in front of the theater, praying and singing. Someone gave us a large cross that lit up and was a symbol of God's power to free people.

There were several times when we were in danger. Once, an angry man stood nearby Doug and threatened him. A state police officer stepped through the crowd in between them and protected Doug. We didn't see him come, and we didn't see how he left. We wondered if he was an angel sent to protect us.

One night in the cold of winter, snowballs came flying at our team. Angry words and threats accompanied those balls of snow. While we couldn't see who threw them, but always suspected that the theater owners were responsible. We prayed for those boys and blessed them. We also prayed for the community of Smithton.

Years later, Gino, our friend from Smithton, told us he was paid to throw the snowballs. He had become a believer, a friend and part of our community at the Christian Center. The Bible says that God makes us more than conquerors, and that was true for Gino.

CHAPTER 22

FISHING

Follow me and I will make you fishers of men.
Matthew 4:19

THE SEVENTH DAY was set aside as a day of rest—the fourth command. Sundays are a time of giving out for Christians in the ministry. There were many reasons the Lord required his people to set aside time. It was to refocus, rest, and give Him our full attention, among others.

Because Sundays were not days of rest, we took Mondays as our Sabbath days. We left our busy lives and spent the day focused on the Lord and our family. We loved to spend Mondays in the mountains and often went to Five Pines to enjoy the beauty of nature and fish. It was restful and restorative to our spirits.

We believed God had Five Pines was a campground with a beautiful lake filled with an abundance of fish. The days we spent there were always refreshing for us. It was a family business. When we would pay our fee at the main lodge, the atmosphere struck us. Campgrounds most often have a family environment, but Five Pines was quite different. It had a bar, and often the person waiting on us had an alcoholic drink in their hands.

While Doug and I were fishing, we would pray for the owners. We asked the Lord for an opportunity to share Jesus with them. We believed God had a plan for our time out there besides trout fishing.

In the fall of 1977, Doug brought a group of Royal Rangers boys on a weekend camping trip. Throughout the weekend, they racked up a significant bill at the camp store. It was a rainy few days, and the group headed home early. When Doug stopped by the camp office to pay, Judy was at the desk.

"What does your shirt say?" She read it aloud. "Jesus Airlift '77. *Jesus te ama*. Is that Spanish?"

"No, Portuguese," Doug replied. "It means 'Jesus loves you.' We spent a month in Brazil this summer telling people about Jesus." Judy seemed fascinated. Doug noticed several new "Jesus" signs around the office and wondered what was happening.

"Judy, we have been coming here to fish for years. My wife and I love to go fishing at the pond on our days off. We have been praying for you and your family while we sit on the shore."

His words seemed to catch her by surprise. "I hope to see you again the next time you come by," she said. Her voice had a shaky tone as if she was fighting back tears.

We could not stop again before we left for YWAM two years later. Often, we remembered that time and wondered what might have happened after that afternoon.

After our season in YWAM, we lived in New Hampshire until 1997. Then we returned to the Pittsburgh area. On one of our days off, we took a rest day back to the mountains and were happy to see the Five Pines sign still on the road. "Let's see if Judy is still there!"

When we pulled onto the property, we noticed many things had changed. There was a Bed and Breakfast at the bottom of the road. New cabins had been added, and the lodge had undergone a renovation. Fishermen with their children lined the pond shore, so that was still an attraction.

The girl who greeted us at the desk was friendly. "Hello, will you be camping?" Doug returned her smile. "We used to come here many years ago when we were first married. It is great to see how nice everything looks after all this time. Is Judy still the owner?"

She seemed surprised that we knew Judy's name. "Oh, yes, Marty and Judy. Do they know you? What is your name? I will call them." She grabbed the phone. "They are at their house at the Quiet House Bed and Breakfast down the road."

I could hear Judy shouting at the other side of the phone. "Doug Tunney! Tell him to stay right there. We are coming." It wasn't a minute later when their truck pulled up in a cloud of dust. Marty and Judy hopped out, and before we knew it, they had thrown their arms around us.

"Thank God for you!" they exclaimed.

Why they were thanking God for us was a mystery. Something happened in their lives that made them happy and grateful.

"Please sit. We have a story to tell you." Marty showed us into the sitting area. "When you told me that Jesus loved me and that you and Deb were praying for our family, I felt tears welling up from my heart. I fell on the floor in the back room and wept for hours. Once, when I was drunk, the enemy told me I would never see the face of God. I wrongly believed that until you shared with me. Your words were a message of hope from God to me."

Marty continued, "My wife was at the lowest point of her life. At thirty-seven, she was unhappy and lonely even though she was surrounded by people. She needed a savior. She met the Lord that day, and it changed her life. Then I found Jesus, and our children, parents, all our employees and their families, and many friends were saved."

"You cannot imagine," Judy interjected. "Many people came to the Lord and were filled with the Holy Spirit. We began baptizing people in our swimming pool, and we dedicated our land and our business to Jesus in March 1978. On Sundays, we closed the campground and have had a church on this property for the past twenty years. God used your words to begin a move of God in this mountain community that has changed the lives of hundreds of people."

God used our time at the fishing pond to fish for men.

CHAPTER 23

INTERCESSION

AFTER HEARING Loren Cunningham teach about intercession at the Charismatic Conference in Pittsburgh, Doug shared with the Power Group Discipleship Group. Intercession differed from how we approached our times of corporate prayer. Waiting on God, coming with a clean heart, and listening for what was in His heart was a revolutionary concept for us.

Often, prayer meetings comprised individuals bringing a grocery list of their personal needs. Many times, the focus was not on agreeing with others but on waiting for the moment you could jump in with your concerns. While we knew God wanted us to bring our needs to him, there were times when we realized we didn't know how to pray (Romans 8:26), and the Holy Spirit led us.

That night, we broke into small groups and listened for God's direction during our prayer time. We entered the prayer time with thanksgiving (Psalm 100) and asked the Holy Spirit to show us anything that would hold us back from hearing from Him.

After a time of waiting, Doug's group shared what they had received during the quiet time. Janet said she had a picture of people in canoes and they were paddling away from danger. Another person said Lake Victoria came to mind. Someone else added, "I think something about Africa." We had never heard of Lake Victoria, so we went to the world map to find it. It was in Uganda.

We prayed for the people who were escaping, asking God to grant them safe passage. Weeks later, Janet read a small article in the New York Times about a group of Christians that were fleeing persecution by Idi Amin in Uganda. They were escaping in dug-out canoes across Lake Victoria into Tanzania.

It was a confirmation that the Lord had guided our prayer time. We adopted that way of praying and listening for God's purposes and plans in our times of intercession.

CHAPTER 24

JESUS '79

OUR REVIVAL church had been through two very traumatic events: a church split and a fallen pastor.

Then winter came—a very harsh winter. Snowfall after snowfall accumulated many feet of snow. We heard that Rich's airplane hangar had collapsed under the weight of the snow. All the planes stored there were damaged. It was a substantial financial loss for him. Our prayers would have been with him a year earlier. We would have done everything to help him.

But not this time. We felt a sense of justice and vindication. Wasn't Rich responsible for ripping apart our church, derailing the revival, and putting ambition above unity? And we looked the other way. We didn't say it, but our hearts had no sadness over his loss—no prayers, encouragement, or offer of help. He deserved it.

Life went on. We put it out of our consciousness and embraced what was ahead. Sometimes I wonder how much trouble we push down and try to keep out of our minds as we refuse to reconcile broken relationships. Time doesn't heal these issues; they will fester until reconciliation and healing occur.

We were preparing to leave for YWAM, and we were at Jesus '79 in Mercer, PA, with the Power Group youth. The grounds of the event were beautiful, and worship filled the air. Thousands of believers were experiencing something of heaven on earth. After the church struggles, I found a refreshing relief there.

I wandered into one of the meeting tents where Iverna Tompkins was speaking. She opened the book of Obadiah. "The Israelites were descendants of Jacob. The Edomites were descendants of Esau. Hundreds of years after the well-known conflicts between these two brothers there was still a huge divide. It was after their tear-filled public restoration. The Israelites were in a valley, and God was bringing judgment against them. An army was attacking them, and they were fleeing to the hills to escape.

"The Edomites were also there on the hillsides and could have come to their aid. But instead of rescuing, they joined the attack and shut off the mountain passes and escape routes. The resentment between these groups still ran deep, so deep that the Edomites rejoiced in the enemy's attack on the Israelites. Instead of helping their brothers, they were part of the attack. God brought a heavy judgment against the Edomites. If you don't forgive from your heart, surface reconciliations, even with tears, will stay with you and poison others, even for generations."

Tears were streaming down my face as I realized I had done the same thing. I was happy when my friend Rich was having such a hard time. I felt vindicated. I spoke the right words in public, but my heart was still bitter, and I withheld any love and support. The story of Obadiah was my heart.

I knelt by my chair in the sawdust and asked God to forgive me and help me extend forgiveness to Rich. The meeting was over, and I wandered out of the tent amid 50,000 people and almost walked right into Rich and Alice. It was no coincidence. God had heard my heart and set up an encounter for reconciliation.

Through my tears, I spoke to them, "Please forgive me."

There was forgiveness on both sides and true restoration. I was so grateful for the restored fellowship; I did not know how significant it would be in the weeks to come.

We left for YWAM in September, and our going-away party was wonderful. Rich came to our church and was the master of ceremonies. Friends from churches and many other groups came to send us off with their love and blessings. Psalm 133 says that God commands his blessing where there is unity. That gathering of friends was one of the very blessed moments of our lives. After our Discipleship Training School in Concord, we went straight to a School of Evangelism in Lausanne, Switzerland. We were so thankful to have mended relationships and to have our hearts free from bitterness.

"Doug, call home, please. There is a serious situation." The school leader told us at the end of a morning lecture.

Doug looked at me when he hung up the phone. His face was drained of color, his words shaky. "Rich has died." He was forty-two, a young man in his prime, and healthy. It was shocking news—the saddest news. We realized how important our reconciliation had been just a few months earlier.

I have learned so many lessons about forgiveness. I commit to never missing an opportunity to extend and receive forgiveness. You don't know how life will turn out, and you might miss the moment God has provided to restore relationships.

PART THREE

Mission Adventures in Youth with a Mission
Concord, New Hampshire
Lausanne, Switzerland
Athens, Greece
Hurlach and Frankford, Germany
Amsterdam, Netherlands

CHAPTER 25

LETTING GO

WE PACKED our bags for YWAM Concord in September 1979, without plans to return home. We sold most of our belongings, except for a library of study books that were boxed and shipped on ahead to YWAM Lausanne, Switzerland.

Our missionary prayer cards declared our eventual destination to be Sudan. We expected we would end up in Africa. After Disciple Training School (DTS) in Concord, New Hampshire, we would head to Lausanne for a five-month School of Evangelism.

In the weeks leading up to our departure, I could see the effects of our decision weighing on my mother because she was very close to our girls. How could I follow God's call on our lives if obedience hurt those closest to me?

There is always a cost to obeying God's call for your life. Sometimes it is in relinquishing material things, releasing the security of being known and loved by friends, or letting go of your dreams and ambitions to embrace God's dream for your life. Relinquishing material things was easy for me. Letting go of my reputation and the community of friends was more difficult. The most challenging cost for me was to let go of what others wanted for my life and deal with the pain that my obedience cost them.

I pulled into the Kroger Food Market in Elizabeth, Pennsylvania, and noticed my parent's car in the lot. It was an older model El Camino with a distinctive look to the paint. I knew it was my mother's, but it surprised me because she had never shopped in that part of town.

Then I noticed something was happening in the store. A woman had collapsed and was lying on the floor. It was my mom lying there, getting emergency help from the staff. My mom could barely put words together to tell me what had happened. Her speech was slurred. She refused to have an ambulance come and agreed to have us help her to my car and then to my home.

"What happened, Mom?"

"I am not sure. I picked up a few groceries on my way home. As I walked through the store, I could hear little children playing in the next aisle. They were laughing. They were young, like your girls. Then I realized you would leave soon and take your children to Europe and Africa. The next thing I knew, I was on the floor. People were trying to help me. I looked up, and you were here."

I took that experience with me as we left for YWAM a few weeks later. My decision to follow God would have not only a personal cost to me but also a personal cost to those I loved and who loved me.

My mother dedicated me to the Lord when I was a toddler. She watched me grow in my faith. After a week at the New Wilmington Missionary Conference when I was fourteen, something new was birthed in my heart. I responded to an invitation to go on missions and gave my information on a card. Our local pastor followed up and visited with a book about missions and a prayer that God would guide my life. My mom now recognized that there was a new challenge for her—surrendering our girls and me to God's purposes.

CHAPTER 26

YWAM CONCORD

WE WERE making plans to take our little family to join YWAM. Our time at the Alliance Chapel had been amazing, and we could see the hand of God. We sent many young people from the Power Group to be trained in ministry. Some went to Wycliffe Bible Translators, some to Christ for the Nations, and many to YWAM in Concord, New Hampshire. Now we were ready to move on to a life of missions. It was exciting, and we told everyone about our plans to go to Sudan and set up a prayer ministry for the world. We would get trained in England, go to Malta, and then go to Sudan. We already had prayer cards printed with this vision.

The first step with Youth with a Mission was Discipleship Training School (DTS). We mailed our DTS applications to England and were assured that it was the right path. We waited for our acceptance letter, and as time passed, we wondered why there was no response. Just a few weeks before the DTS was to begin, we had to buy our plane tickets. Then the letter came, but it was not what we expected. There had been a mail strike in England, and our application had been held up. There was no space for families left. "Sorry, and I hope things work out," was the reply we got.

We had resigned from our positions as youth pastors. We had told everyone by faith that we were on our way to Africa via England. Our plans had hit a brick wall. Were we presumptuous again? We called Nick Savoca, our friend from YWAM in Concord.

"England's loss is Concord's gain!" Nick said. He encouraged us to plan toward joining him there.

Most of the Concord staff were young people we had discipled in the Power Group. The young people we had sent into missions would lead us.

This detour took us to a place of humility and leadership lessons that only God could have planned for us.

In the four decades since, we have never stepped foot in YWAM England or found a calling in Sudan. But we learned how to serve under younger and less experienced leaders. We embraced a change of plans and God-ordained detours. We learned how to deal with people's opinions about our mistakes in guidance. And today, we can see how God set us up with this experience and called us to have our roots planted deep in New England soil that would fill half of our lives.

After the three-month lecture phase of DTS in Concord, we skipped the outreach and headed for Lausanne, Switzerland.

CHAPTER 27

FISHKILL

DONNA AND Mark Britt, our friends, picked us up at the YWAM base in Concord, New Hampshire, at the end of our DTS lecture phase. We were to visit with our family and friends in the Mon Valley before we headed to YWAM in Switzerland and an outreach in Europe.

The twelve-hour drive on Christmas Eve was full of conversation. We had so much to share from all that had happened in our lives during the past three months. Our girls, Rachel and Bethany, were asleep in the way back. Doug and Mark had dozed off in the back seat. It was a perfect scenario for catching up with Donna.

"Our lives belong to the Lord, 100 percent. Everything we have is for His Glory!" I proclaimed.

"Right, everything!" Donna replied.

"We don't care about having material things," I continued. "It is all going to burn, anyway."

"You are so right," she again agreed.

"Everything, even things like this car," I added, though it wasn't mine. "It is a nice car, but we don't care about cars!"

Before Donna could agree, we heard a loud noise from the engine. Her foot was on the gas, but the car lost all its power, and she could barely drift onto the berm of the highway.

Mark and Doug had the hood up in a minute, and their unprofessional diagnosis was simple. The engine was dead. Suddenly, my proclamation that we didn't care about cars seemed to miss our current state. The Britts' car wasn't going anywhere. It was Christmas Eve. We were six hours from our family, and none of us had more than a few dollars. The material things I just said didn't matter now seemed to matter a lot.

"Mom, Dad, where are we? Are we almost at Grandma's?" Rachel shouted from the way back. Our little girls had awakened.

"Everything is going to be okay. We stopped for a break," I told them, not knowing if everything would be okay.

We did what came naturally in a crisis. We prayed, "Lord, help us." I added, "Sorry about saying the car didn't matter."

There was a phone booth alongside the road, and it had a three-inch-thick Yellow Pages phone book—a Fishkill, New York phone directory. We gathered some quarters together to make calls for help. *Ring, ring, ring.* Garages were not open at dinner time on Christmas Eve.

Who do we call for help? I took the Yellow Pages directory and began to call churches. Surely someone would rescue us—a missionary family stranded on Christmas Eve. As soon as I said hello, click! They hung up. It happened over and over. Apparently, the churches were not ready to rescue us. Maybe they thought we were prank-calling them.

"Keep trying!" Doug encouraged me.

"Mom, we are cold," added the girls.

I tried another number, and this time there was a response. "Hello, this is Mary from First Baptist Church. How may I help you?"

I was so surprised and thankful that it took me a second to respond. I shared our story with her, and she said, "We will pick you up right away. We are having a special church dinner and meeting tonight, so please join us."

They called us their "Christmas travelers." One member had a car rental business and handed us the keys to a car. After a delicious meal, the church prayed for us and sent us on our way with an offering for gas. They would make sure the Britts' car was towed and repaired. We had been rescued again; it was a reminder that God was watching over us and would always take care of us.

CHAPTER 28

LAUSANNE

OUR THREE months in DTS were over, and we boarded a plane for Switzerland. Our new home for the next three months was the YWAM Lausanne hotel. It was a beautiful setting, with the majestic Swiss Alps in the distance and a pine forest surrounding the property. Our class of thirty was from nine nations. I experienced grief for what we left behind and the uncertainty of what lay ahead.

Every afternoon, Doug would watch the girls, and I would retreat to a quiet place in the basement of the YWAM hotel, where there was a sauna. A locked door provided a quiet place to think, pray, and cry. Every day, I did all three. "Help me let go and trust you." Each day, I asked again.

His answer came through the Bible:

> Listen, daughter, and pay careful attention: Forget your people and your father's house. Let the king be enthralled by your beauty; honor him, for he is your lord.
> Psalm 45:10–11 NIV

I knew God was with me in the hidden sauna room. Forget what is behind: your own people and your father's house. God wants to be your focus and the Lord of your heart.

That evening, our speaker was Reona Peterson (Joly). The story of her journey into Albania was amazing. "Tomorrow, you die!" was her testimony message. Then she said, "I want to tell you about God's call to me to leave my family and life in New Zealand. He spoke to me from Psalm 45:10–11."

Her testimony encouraged the other students. I was stunned to have her share the exact verses from Psalm 45 that I had read in the sauna just hours before. God was speaking to my heart. It was apparent that it was no coincidence. It was also a battle for my heart.

As I headed for the sauna the next afternoon, I had those words from Psalm 45 running through my mind. I brought my Bible, and a book called *Those Who Love Him* by Basilea Schlink.

That day, when I closed the sauna door behind me, I pondered Psalm 45 from the day before. I picked up the book I had brought and turned to a new chapter using the bookmark I had left. There, on the next page, were these verses in italics:

"Hearken, O daughter, and consider, and incline thine ear; forget also thine own people, and thy father's house...."
Psalm 45

God was speaking to me. I realized that Jesus also had to embrace His Father's will, which had a cost. At the cross, those who were dearest to Him were there. His mother, Mary, John, and other women who were His followers were there. They were experiencing the full impact of His obedience.

My obedience to God's call in my life would have consequences. The ripples of my life would affect others, and some would suffer because of it. There was no turning back.

The Lord asked me to let go to embrace what was ahead.

What was I holding on to—comfort, reputation, fear, and loved ones? While I was very clear about what God was saying to me, I was less clear about how to respond.

Several days later, my Dutch friend, Pauline, visited me in our apartment. Our housing was next to the YWAM hotel. Pauline was a student at the School of Evangelism with me. I was drawn to her because of her love for the Lord.

"Deb, what is this photo about?" She was referring to a framed picture of our Power Group youth fellowship from our previous ministry.

She asked me, "Why is this on your nightstand?"

My answer only made her more curious. "Isn't that what God has asked you to surrender to follow Him?" she asked. I nodded.

"Maybe it isn't wise to remind yourself daily of past successes and ask God to point your heart toward what lies ahead for you?" She challenged me.

When I tucked the photograph away in our luggage, I realized it was a small step of obedience to embrace an even deeper relationship with the Lord.

CHAPTER 29

STRENGTH AND WEAKNESS

"GOOD MORNING. I want to invite you to live all out for the Lord,"
the speaker shared. "I've decided to spend my lecture time discussing
my failures."

The room was silent. For the next few hours, we heard about
mistakes, sins, failures, disappointments, God's grace, and much
more. For me, that was one of the most affecting lectures during our
missionary training in Lausanne, Switzerland.

I learned good people struggle. People who are called must deal
with their own limits and human failings. Loved people face the
reality that not everyone will love them. Unmistakable followers of
Jesus bear the mark of perseverance and breaking as part of their
qualifications for greater service. During times of struggle in our lives,
I often reached back to this moment and found encouragement in the
fact that we were not alone.

CHAPTER 30

THE ROAD TO ATHENS

OUR TIME in Lausanne for our School of Evangelism went by so fast. Soon we were traveling across Europe in a Mercedes bus with the school staff and other students, a trailer full of luggage in tow behind us. The students filled every seat on the bus with no room to stretch their legs. Often, people were lying in the aisles to get some sleep.

A few hours into our journey, we saw the beautiful Alps ahead. The road had a distinct incline as the engine responded to pull our bus full of missionaries and our trailer up through the mountain passes. Beautiful, heavy snow fell. Quickly, the road was covered with dense snow and just one set of tire tracks ahead of us.

We were told that our bus driver, Russ, was an experienced driver. I wondered how "experienced" he could be at twenty-one years of age. My faith had to be in the *Lord's* protection, not *Russ's* qualifications. Boxes of Bibles and Christian literature filled the cargo holds of the bus, which added to the weight.

As we rounded a turn in the road, you could feel the tires slip. Up ahead, a semi-truck had stopped at an angle, almost blocking the whole road. Most of us were dozing. Conversations had quieted down to a few whispers.

Russ shifted gears to get more traction. Despite our tires spinning to take us forward, I saw we were slipping backward. My heart started pumping, and I looked around for how we could get out before we slid over the mountain's edge. People were sleeping in the aisles. We were fifteen rows away from the exit door.

"We are sliding! Russ!!!" He didn't respond to the screams but put the emergency brake on, grabbed four-wheel chocks, and jumped out of the bus. I could see him sliding, but he got the wedges under the tires on both sides. The bus stopped. I could not imagine those chocks being enough to hold us, but they did. Eventually, the road ahead was cleared, and we continued to Greece.

We began our outreach with a quick prayer for protection, and I added to those prayers dozens of times on our journey to Athens.

It was 1980, and Yugoslavia was a communist country with many Slavic territories. The nation collapsed in 2003. Our trip would go through the countryside. Many international students expressed concerns and demanded they travel across borders. We had two South Africans, Villy and Villica, and they were scared because communist countries opposed their nation.

Before we got to the border, our leaders warned us not to say anything when the guards came aboard. "Hand your passports and any documents they ask for. Let the leaders answer questions. Be polite. Pray. Say nothing!"

Armed soldiers stopped us at the crossing, and a guard came on the bus. He asked each of us to hand our passports to him. He looked us over and moved on to the next person. There were no smiles. I could hear my heart beating in the silence. He took the stack of passports for processing. Each one would need a validation stamp.

After thirty minutes, he returned with the same stern face and stepped onto the bus. He handed the passports to Russ. He held on to Villy and Villica's documents and announced, "Your group may enter the country, except for these two. They must get out!"

Russ replied, "Our group is from nine nations. We are a team. We are not leaving anyone behind." The guard walked away, and we were not going anywhere. An hour passed; then after another hour, the guard returned with the two passports. His other hand stretched out as if asking for money. Russ put some bills in his hand. He tossed the passports on the floor of the bus and motioned for us to drive through the gate.

Villy and Villica got their passports, but when they looked inside, there was no stamp. They were now in a communist country with no proof they could have legally entered. In a few days, we would have to leave through another border without documents. Would they be arrested?

On the travel through the country we prayed. A half mile from the exit checkpoint, we stopped along the road. It was the only way out. We realized how serious it could be, and we had no plan if the border police stopped us.

Tap. Ping. Tap, tap, tap. Drops of rain started hitting the windshield with escalating intensity. Thunder and lightning filled the air.

It had been clear skies one minute, and now it was a torrential downpour; the rain was coming in sideways sheets. We could hardly see a foot ahead of us as we rolled to a stop at the guard house.

No one uttered a word. The storm was the only noise echoing through the bus and filling our thoughts. We waited for the guard. No one came out. A soldier put his hand out of the window and waved us through. No questions. Nothing checked. As suddenly as the rain started, it stopped on the other side of the border.

We knew the Lord had made a way. No one could doubt God had a plan for our team to reach Athens.

CHAPTER 31

ATHENS

OUR MERCEDES bus pulled up to Camping Varkiza in Athens. It was the first stop for our outreach. Some of the outreach team would go on to the 1980 Olympics in Russia. A smaller team stayed in Athens for the next three months. It had been weeks since we ventured out from Lausanne, Switzerland, with the staff and students from our School of Evangelism.

Greece has beautiful coastlines, and our picturesque campground was on the Mediterranean Sea. We unloaded our luggage and grabbed a tent. I took Rachel and Bethany for a walk down to the water while Doug set up our three-room canvas home. The sea was crystal clear. Standing still, we could see small tropical fish swimming along the shoreline.

The next few months would be testing. Leaving our home in Western Pennsylvania was a step of faith for us. Our family had immigrated from Europe and settled in the Mon Valley. We had deep roots there. I lived there from preschool through college, and during our first ministry position with the Alliance Chapel was there. It provided a sense of belonging to have friends and be part of the community. Now, we were part of a large team from many nations, living in a tent on the shore of the Mediterranean Sea. I fell asleep each night, wrestling with the loneliness, far away from everything I had known.

There were no phones except in the camp office. We could make calls to our loved ones back home at a high cost for a missionary. Once you put your order in for a call, you waited. Sometimes the wait was more than an hour while overseas operators connected you across the Atlantic.

Our food was prepared and served community-style as the YWAMers lined up outside. I had a plastic bucket with a bowl and would bring our meals "home" to our tent. Our family tent had two small rooms to sleep in and a living area with a plastic window to see the outside world.

It was a challenge to make this place a home for our family. Our money had dwindled to just a few dollars. We had a 15-watt light bulb in our tent. At night, I would put the girls to bed and write letters home under the dim light. My longing for home was deep. I struggled to find my identity apart from the ministry. Each day, I felt more unknown and useless.

Doug was always resourceful, and it didn't take long for him to see that we needed to transform our tent into an actual home. One morning, he came up from the shore with pieces of broken crates in his arms and a smile on his face. He fashioned a table and four chairs from these discarded boards and wire. We went to the market and bought a red and white tablecloth that added a finishing touch to our new dining room. Each day, I would walk along the hill with the girls and pick wildflowers for our table. I now had a place to call home, a space to invite friends for a meal and fellowship.

Doug joined the outreach team and headed to the fishing area called Piraeus. That was a unique time in Greece. Don Stephens, one of our international leaders, was detained for sharing the Gospel. He would later have to answer for his actions in court with the possibility of a jail sentence.

Piraeus was a seaport teeming with sailors. It was a landing point for Africans who had worked on ships and whose contracts ended when they arrived in Athens.

Greek law limited the foreign sailors' opportunity to get jobs once they finished their tour of duty. Ninety percent of the new hires had to be Greeks, so thousands of international sailors were stranded there.

Doug and the YWAM team would take our Mercedes bus to the seaport in the evenings. They shared the Gospel and invited sailors onto the bus for a time of fellowship and teaching. The bus was full each night. Lord Adams, from The Gambia, joined with the sailors each night.

Sailors were coming to the Lord! Those were the firstfruits of our ministry in Athens. It was an answer to our prayers. Everyone was glad. Everything seemed fine until we learned that the new believers lived a significantly compromised life. Times were hard for them all. Each night, the sailors scraped together all their funds, and one would rent a room. Then, ten to fifteen others would sneak in and sleep there.

The jobs they were waiting for were scarce. The hiring representative always expected a bribe for a job on the ship. No one expected to get a job without a bribe. When one sailor was called for an interview, the others would pool their funds together to help him with a bribe.

It was a tough moment when Doug explained to them that following Christ means obedience and trust in God instead of faith in their means. "Following Jesus means obeying His commands. It means honesty and putting aside deception and lying. When your trust is in God, you cannot compromise."

The bus was silent. One by one, the sailors got up and walked out. It was a sort of reverse altar call. No one stayed on the bus except the YWAMers.

Our team wrapped up the night without uttering a word. "Maybe we should just have avoided that subject, Doug." Yet they knew a true disciple had to embrace the cross and trust God in every area of their lives. Following Jesus also meant living with integrity and being trustworthy.

For the following days, the team would sit on the bus, waiting for the sailors to join, but no one came. Counting the cost is a pause that shapes your destiny.

After a week, the men returned. They were smiling, and it was as if everything was supposed to be okay again. "Please, let's not talk about the bribes or the lies. Let's just talk about the Bible." But Doug and the team knew it was a turning point for them. In love, they reminded them that their lives must change as they follow Christ.

The uneasy silence had returned. Doug noticed Isaac had tar on his clothes. As he stood up, everyone listened. "I have tar marks from where I slept last night. I will no longer lie about paying for a room. I slept on the dock. I won't let fear rule my life and will not pay a bribe. I decided to follow Jesus."

The others looked on, shocked at hearing those words. There was a mumble amongst them. They thought his unreasonable proclamation of faith would doom him. He challenged the other sailors to join him. Now he had made Christ his Savior and the Lord of his life.

No one joined him.

"Did you hear the news? Isaac has a job interview tomorrow!" One sailor shouted as our bus pulled in the next day. Everyone knew the interviewer would expect a bribe. His words of faith would be tested. Our team prayed. I am sure the other sailors wondered.

He arrived for the interview with a desperate prayer. Could God be trusted? Would he continue to follow Jesus if they denied him a position? Would he turn back?

As he sat down, there were familiar questions about experience and availability. Then there was the expected question. "How much do you want this job? What are you willing to give to secure it?"

He sat quietly. Forming his words, silently praying, he replied, "I have followed Jesus and believe that God has called me to be an honest man, faithful to my words, and I cannot pay a bribe for this job."

The silence was awkward and long. Then, in the most amazing turn of events, the interviewer replied, "You are hired. In my business, so many men begin their service on these ships dishonestly. Bribes are a part of their lives. I see you are an honest man and would be a valuable part of our crew."

That night on the bus, the others waited to hear his report. He pulled out of his pocket a neatly folded piece of paper, a contract for a job on a ship. "I got a job, and I trusted Jesus and did not pay a bribe." This was a stunning moment. It was a breakthrough that would change all of their lives.

> *We overcome by the blood of the lamb and the word of our testimony.*
> Revelation 12:11

He was now an overcomer with a new job and a powerful story of God's faithfulness.

Then another surprise—another sailor stood up. "I have decided to follow Jesus." Then another. The joy expressed among us all was so honest and real. Salvation had come to these amazing men, who now trusted Jesus as Savior and Lord.

In the months ahead, one by one, we would hear of them getting jobs without bribes, and they became known as the Christians who could be trusted. Lord Adams was one of them.

CHAPTER 32

CONFLICT IN ATHENS

WHILE DOUG spent his evenings with the sailors in Piraeus, the girls and I had our nightly routine: prayers to end our day and a conversation about the blessings of each day. Counting blessings helped to keep our hearts focused and thankful.

Adjusting to camping was difficult. The sun beat down on us through the day until we found a place of shade. Our daughters would rest for naps on the granite countertops in the laundry area. The girls found it hard to settle down in the noisy campground. Routine tasks were challenging. Our clothes became more tinted with the red dirt of the camp. We did our laundry in the small, three-inch-deep sink in the bathroom. I rinsed our clothes in a bucket the best I could and hung them on a clothesline. Random people would walk through the camp, and often our clothes would be stolen while they hung to dry.

Our meals were prepared for the entire outreach team in a cook tent. Most days, simple meals were prepared. It was often local vegetables in a soup. After a month, our team was around thirty. Most of the 300 YWAMers left for Russia for the Olympic outreach. Laura was our cook. She was a native of the Caribbean.

Since leaving our home in September, I had had no spiritual responsibility. My focus was to care for my little family. Russ, our team leader asked me to lead a small intercessory group. This was a welcomed opportunity to pray with these five girls and I was happy to have something to do.

Laura was in my group. We began our time of prayer, and I noticed Laura seemed agitated, irritated to be with us, and she was making it known that she would not cooperate.

"Laura, is everything okay?" I asked her.

"No, everything is not okay," she responded. "Why do I have to be here? You are an American, and I have no respect for Americans. You know nothing about following God. You don't have faith."

I was very surprised at her reaction. She didn't know me and she was judging me harshly. Every day we gathered to pray Each day she would come, but she ignored us the whole time.

Our meals were prepared and served from the cook tent. Each day, I waited in line with my red bucket to gather food for our family. I was thankful for the dining table and chairs that Doug had made. That night, Laura looked my way and caught me straight in her gaze. I looked down to avoid a negative comment, and she snarled, "I can't believe I have to be in your group." I gulped. "And by the way, your children are terrible, so loud and unlikeable."

That was beyond what I could deal with. I looked the other way and was determined to never speak with her again. My little girls, Rachel and Bethany (five and three) were so precious. They never complained. It wasn't easy for them to be away from their family and friends. The few toys they brought in their small backpacks were broken or worn out. The summer heat even made it difficult for them to be outside to play. They didn't know it was the trip of a lifetime, but they were handling things pretty well.

Laura's words hurt me. I could take the insults she threw at me during prayer time, but she was insulting my family, my little girls. I hoped they would never hear such words from an adult, especially from someone in ministry.

I never spoke to her again. My heart burned with bitterness, and I ignored her as much as possible. I walked into the cook tent one day, not realizing she was there.

"Oh, Hi," I said, trying to be friendly, "I see you are preparing dinner."

"Never speak to me again," she replied. "I don't like you. I don't like your family. I never want you to even come into this tent." Her reaction shocked me.

The weeks of holding in the hurt from her words were over. The frustration boiled over, and I shouted back, "You must never say things about my family." She shouted louder, and I reciprocated. Our conflict was echoing through the campground.

One of the YWAM guys looked in the tent to calm us down. "Ladies, we are supposed to be witnesses here." We didn't acknowledge him or his message. I was shocked at the anger I felt, and I grabbed her shoulders, looked straight into her eyes, and finished the conflict with a threat that she should never speak to my children again.

We never spoke to each other again throughout the entire trip back to Switzerland. She went to Holland. My husband and I planned to return to Athens to join the Anastasis, the YWAM ship. We changed our plans when the ship was taken into dry dock and could no longer house families. A door opened for us to volunteer in Amsterdam.

The last thing I wanted to do was end up in Holland and see Laura again. Upon arriving in Amsterdam, one of the first things I did was ask if anyone knew Laura. I asked if she was living in the city. Sensing my concern, the staff assured me she lived in the countryside at Heidebeek. I was relieved.

Weeks passed, and they announced that all the YWAMers would go to Heidebeek for a special time of fellowship. That included Doug, me, and our girls, and that would include Laura.

The visit to Heidebeek was great. Several hundred missionaries from all the bases in Holland were there. It was a giant homecoming, with music and delicious food but, thankfully, no Laura. I scanned the meeting room several times throughout the day, dreading her arrival. Someone mentioned that Laura was not feeling well and would not attend the meeting. That was the best news for me. I feared meeting her again. It had been months since our encounter in the cook tent, and I still felt guilty for my reaction.

As the evening was ending, I caught a glimpse of her. The old feelings flooded back to me. Her words began playing through my mind. She seemed especially at home and greeted people as she walked through the hall.

I planned to exit before she could notice me, but then the thought came—*you must forgive, and you must ask for forgiveness.* I had learned that lesson before, but it was different this time. It wasn't my battle, but it was about injustice for how she had treated my family.

I hesitantly walked up to her. She walked away, and I just said, "I am sorry, really sorry." Tears flowed down my cheeks, and I could see she was crying, too.

"I am sorry, too," she cried. "I do not know why I was so mean to you and your family. Please forgive me."

I was sure that part of the reason God had sent us back to Amsterdam was to reconcile with Laura. Relationships are always first in God's heart. I learned some of her story and understood the pain that might have influenced her to treat me like she did. Forgiveness and grace are priorities in God's heart.

CHAPTER 33

DOLLS

"YOU'RE TAKING your children to the mission field?"

People often posed this question to us with a subtle underlying message: that might not be the best idea. We never considered if it was a safe idea when God led us to leave our life in Western Pennsylvania to embrace our calling as missionaries. We were a family with a mission, and our children were a vital part of everything we did.

In September 1979, we took a bold step to leave our family, friends, and ministry and embrace a new direction in missions. Our first stop was YWAM Concord, then Europe.

Downsizing our lives to four suitcases and four backpacks was a challenge. Our daughters, Rachel and Bethany, were five and three. The discussion about what they wished to bring with them was almost impossible.

"You each have a special backpack you chose for this trip, girls. Look through your things. Decide what books and toys you would like to bring with you."

At their ages, they couldn't imagine what life would be like on the mission field. A home with a yard and their own bedroom full of clothes, books, and toys was normal. When we stepped onto the Continental jet to Switzerland, their backpacks were as full as the zippers would allow. They had books, dolls, and other special things that reminded them of their home.

After three months in Lausanne, we began our bus trip to Athens. Most of the toys and books had been worn by then. A few things had been lost, and their dolls were in awful shape. The Mediterranean Sea in Athens was a beautiful place. The girls loved to play in the water at the shoreline. Our tent had three rooms, and they kept their things in the space that they called their "hideout." After a few weeks, though, they complained about wanting new toys.

I thanked God daily for all the ways our family was blessed. Our glass was more than half full, but our girls were well aware of the empty part.

Our girls developed a heart for prayer and cared for the refugee children. They heard God speak to them during intercession with other children. One time, at the Concord base, they prayed for children in camps who were getting hurt falling out of their bunk beds. We later learned that the camps had beds stacked five high, and it was a grave danger for children who tumbled out. They had heard from the Lord, who specifically answered their prayers.

They grew up in so many ways, experiencing other cultures, learning about people who spoke different languages, and enjoying new foods. These were all blessings I was thankful for.

Yet, the thing that most filled their minds was new toys. So we prayed for new toys. Doug and I didn't have extra funds to buy them, so we depended on God's provision.

Hearing their simple and trusting prayers warmed my heart and scared me, too. What if, after their most sincere requests, their prayers seem to go unanswered? I didn't have any way of helping God out on that one, which is how we should live all of our lives. God doesn't need our help to answer our prayers. But I backed them up with prayers of my own.

We spent our days reaching out in Athens and doing home meetings where Christians could invite nonbelievers into their homes for a meal and share about Jesus. Evie was one of our hosts. We hopped on the bus from our campground into the city. We had a long walk from the bus stop to her home, but it was worth it. Her house was full of hospitality, abundant food, and friends. Many people came to Jesus as we shared the Gospel in her living room. Evie's daughter was five, and my girls played with her even though she spoke no English and they spoke no Greek. Friendship transcends language if you lead with your heart.

After a great night of sharing, we had begun our walk to the bus when we heard Evie hail us down with a loud shout. "Wait! I have something for your girls!"

My little ladies turned with Christmas morning excitement and anticipation to see Evie running after us carrying a present. They opened the gift together. It was a beautiful baby doll. Their smiles were very broad as they both held on to part of this one doll as we walked along.

Back at camp, I realized one doll for two girls was a prescription for many conflicts, so I asked them to pray. "Ask God who should have this doll and let's ask him to provide another." Rachel and Bethany went into their tent room and, after a few minutes, emerged with the same answer. This doll would belong to Rachel. Rachel was smiling, and Bethany was sobbing. We prayed for another doll.

Just days later, we were at another home outreach. As the evening finished, Esther, one of our new friends, told us, "Please wait; I have something for your daughters." The anticipation was so much deeper this time because of their struggle and obedience. She handed another baby doll to Bethany.

The doll story will go down to show God's love for our family and His provision. And the remarkable ability of children to hear God's voice, and that even if we must wait, the Lord will hear our hearts' cries.

Our children worked with us, played with us, and heard our conversations over dinner, even when we didn't know they were listening. So, we committed to not having a different conversation when we hoped they were listening and when we hoped they weren't. We wanted to have integrity in our lives.

In times of abundance, we all rejoiced together. When we had needs, we prayed. While we didn't want to burden our kids, we also didn't hide when we had a need. That was difficult because if your kids know you are praying for your daily needs and they go unmet, they could develop a lack of trust in God's character.

But taking the risk of letting them know God is our provider no matter what and including them in asking for our needs also has a high payoff. When God comes through, they will never have to doubt his love and care. Even in times of struggle, they will look for Him.

Watching my children develop their faith was very hard on my heart. I wanted to rescue them from disappointment, but I am so thankful that the Lord used those times to show His faithfulness. I remember reading the writing journal of one of our sons, Jeremy, when he was in the third grade. There was an entry about praying for the money to pay our bills. When I read that, I initially felt embarrassed that he wrote that. We never burdened our children with praying for bills, but I am sure he overheard some conversation, and it became part of his prayer. It was also part of his spiritual inheritance to watch God always provide for us and to know we looked to the Lord for every area of our lives.

Children were never meant to carry grownup burdens and responsibilities. As part of a family, they grow up understanding hard work results in rewards. Yet God is their ultimate provider.

CHAPTER 34

ON THE LAWN

THE TELEX READ, "Ship cannot take families."

"I'm hitchhiking back to Hurlach, Doug. I cannot believe this is happening. Every single thing is so hard." I was blinking back tears as I slumped into the chair.

Another door closed, and hope deferred makes the heart sad. Our plans were being altered at every fork in the road, and now this door was closed. On our way to Africa, we had planned to do our training in England. The door closed, and we ended up in Concord, New Hampshire. The next steps would be to travel to Switzerland, Greece and Germany, and then to return to Athens to serve on the Anastasis, YWAM's mercy ship, and to Malta and Sudan.

Our travels throughout Europe had exhausted us and exhausted our finances. With each move, funds from home had missed us, and we were down to our last few dollars.

Doug had hitched a ride with a van carrying relief supplies headed for Athens and the ship. We waited in Hurlach, Germany, waiting for finances to join him. Halfway through Europe, he received word that the ship could not take families.

When Doug arrived at the castle, the leaders asked for a meeting. "Unfortunately, your rooms are reserved for a family that arrives on Thursday for language study. We hadn't mentioned it before because you were leaving." I took a deep breath and held back tears. "We are so sorry. Make plans. If all else fails, you may sleep on the library floor until you figure out where to go. You must pack and have everything out of your rooms before they arrive in two days."

This matter-of-fact comment seemed to be business as usual for them, but for us, it was devastating. The door to the ship was closed, and our future was as dark as night.

We prayed. We asked for suggestions. There were no suggestions, except for again the library floor.

Then, a staff girl mentioned the possibility of serving at a new YWAM location in Amsterdam. They needed workers to renovate the Samaritan's Inn. We inquired to see if they would welcome us and our family. The reply was "Yes."

Finally, an open door, hundreds of miles away. We had no way to get there and no funds.

Thursday morning came, and we packed our bags and dragged them to the front lawn of the castle. Bethany's birthday was the next day, and I didn't know what was worse: being stranded in a foreign country or having nothing to celebrate Bethany's birthday. I knew what was worse: having to explain to a four-year-old that we couldn't have a birthday cake or presents.

"Where are we going, Mom?" our girls asked repeatedly. We distracted them. Another group had arrived at the castle: Toymaker, and Son performing arts team. Colin Harbinson, the leader, had children, and they played with our girls on the lawn. The children enjoyed their time and seemed to have no concern for what was happening. After all, their parents had it under control, but we did not.

As the day wore on, my heart sank deeper into despair. I could accept the library, but I could not accept disappointing our little girl.

Before dinner, a van pulled up near us. "Are you the American family that's heading to Holland? We are on our way to the border. Load up."

What a surprising provision. It took little effort to load up since everything we possessed was in four suitcases stacked on the lawn.

CHAPTER 35

AMSTERDAM

THE LONG DRIVE gave me time to worry and wonder. We didn't even know where we were going. The border? Our driver spoke very little English.

Late into the evening, we pulled up to a house, a typical Dutch house, furnished with flowers on the table. They offered us a warm bowl of soup and then led us to our room. "On your way to Amsterdam? The train leaves early tomorrow. You can buy your tickets at the train station."

It was a small but cozy room with feather blankets and soft lights. Bethany reminded us that her birthday was in the morning. "I'm so excited. I will be four!" I didn't need to be reminded.

We gathered on our beds and prayed as a family, committing our day to the Lord, thanking Him for providing our ride, and thanking Him for caring for us. I turned off the light. I lay quietly, confused, afraid, hopeful, and frustrated, all at the same time.

None of our YWAM hosts knew they would bring us to the train station in the morning without money to buy a ticket; no one except our heavenly father, who had things under control. I hoped.

Tap, tap. I opened the door to a smiling German-speaking girl who spoke in simple English. "God put you in my heart. This will help you on your way." She put money in my hand and hugged me.

Shortly after, there was another *tap, tap.* "I couldn't sleep. I wanted to give you some money from the Lord."

Several more visitors came through the night. In the morning, we had enough for our train ride and an extra twenty dollars for a birthday party.

Our new friends dropped us off at the train station early in the morning on September 20, Bethany's birthday. She turned four, and the Lord had not forgotten her. As the train rolled over the countryside, we wondered what would be ahead of us in Amsterdam. All we knew was Doug could help with renovations to the Samaritans Inn.

The train station in Amsterdam was bustling. We made our way outside. A canal went straight through the main city street. Bikes were chained along the metal fences. All the bikes were black. Doug told me that was to keep them from being stolen. If they all look alike, then no one would steal your bike.

We pulled our luggage off the train. They told us it was a short walk to Sam's Inn, but in what direction? We found our way to the outreach center. A very warm Dutch YWAMer met us at the entry door. "Welkom! I am Frank."

We were exhausted from the early morning van trip and long train ride. "May I help you?" Frank now spoke in English, as he understood we were Americans.

"We spoke with George yesterday, and he said you needed help and that we could stay at the inn."

He looked confused. "Again, who did you talk to?"

Doug reached for a folded piece of paper tucked in his Bible. "George."

He looked more confused. "Hmm, George is on vacation and didn't tell us you were coming. This is a problem; we have no room for a family here. Let me talk to someone."

There was no room again. I tried to hide the tears in my red eyes, but I am sure he noticed. Frank suggested we could stay on the floor in the library. That would have been the same suggestion if we had stayed in Hurlach. Apparently, the library was the go-to place for extra visitors at YWAM bases.

What were we to do? It was Bethany's birthday, so we went shopping. With the extra twenty dollars, we found a store with a children's department. Bethany picked out a doll, and we found a Dutch-made cake for our party.

We invited the YWAMers to her party. It didn't seem to matter to Bethany that the guests were not family or friends. We wanted Bethany to know we loved and celebrated her.

"Happy Birthday to you! Happy Birthday to you!" Our Dutch-adopted friends sang along with us.

"American travelers, we have worked things out. We have a flat for you to stay in." Frank was excited to tell us the news. "Hurry, we have a van waiting to take you to Hermi's place, near the Albert Culp Market. She received Jesus with one of our outreach teams. Hermi wants to move into the inn so she can be discipled, and she suggested you stay in her home."

Our van driver was Helmut, and he navigated the narrow streets of Amsterdam with confidence and a lot of speed. I held on to the girls. We could see the Albert Culp Market on our left and a McDonald's ahead of us on the right. The van took a sharp right turn down a very dimly lit street.

"This is the place. Don't be worried. God will protect you."

When someone introduces a new place and says, "Don't be worried," I think there is much to worry about! I looked at Doug with a message in my eyes: I cannot believe you have dragged me to this place!

I smiled at Helmut as he helped us unload our luggage. I tried to tune out the music and shouts from the bar across the street. "Don't be worried," I whispered to myself, but I was anxious.

When he opened the door, there was a mad scrambling of some small animals through the room. In a second, a crash and then silence. "Oh, that was her cats. They are afraid of people, so there is a cat door in the kitchen for them to escape. Hermi warned us they bite, so don't pet them."

I tucked the girls into bed. I handed Bethany her new doll. We prayed, "Thank you, Lord, for our new, temporary home."

Our bedroom had a huge storefront window. My head lay on the pillow about a foot away from the street. The bar's noise never quieted down until the middle of the night. "Doug, I think I heard a gunshot. Tomorrow morning, we are going to the airport and flying home. I don't care that we have no money for a flight. I don't know how we will get to the airport. Promise me we will be on a plane. Or, ask God for a miracle to help me not to worry."

Our girls woke up early and investigated the interesting parts of the flat. The cats had journeyed into the kitchen. When they saw us, they scurried outside in a microsecond.

In an unexplainable turn of events, in my heart, I felt peace. Peace to be in Amsterdam. Peace to live in a flat on a dark street next to a bar. Peace to have scary cats as housemates. And a peace that God had a purpose for these next months and that my life was again surrendered to His will.

After a year in Europe through Switzerland, Greece, Germany, and now Holland, we sensed it was time to head home. We had lived in fourteen places in those eighteen months. In the three months since we arrived in Amsterdam, we had made great friends, and Doug enjoyed his construction work in the Inn. Our leaders in Amsterdam encouraged us, and the community there took an offering to help us with our airfare to go home. We still needed $500 more for the airfare.

We were trusting. Our financial support from our home church had been inconsistent, and we didn't know where to turn for the rest of the funds. When you live in another country and have no resources, $500 is a lot of money. We prayed and gave our situation to the Lord. He was our hope.

We were sitting at lunch in the Samaritan's Inn dining area when we heard voices in the main room. Guests were constantly stopping by. But this time, we heard our names and recognized the voice as our friend from Piraeus, Greece. Lord Adams had found his way to Amsterdam. They hired him for a sailing job without paying a bribe. His ship was docked in the Amsterdam port. He wondered if there was a YWAM base there and if Doug Tunney might be at that base. We were shocked to see him and overjoyed to find him still living for Jesus. How wonderful that he found us!

He brought a Muslim friend, and Doug shared Christ with him. Then Lord Adams looked at us and asked, "Doug, what do you need?" There were some moments of silence as Doug tried to think about what he should tell him.

"Our family needs $500 to finish paying for our airfare to return home." In 1980, that was a lot of money, and for a sailor, that was a month's wages. Lord Adams reached into his pocket and pulled out $500, saying God had spoken to his heart to meet this need for us.

In Athens, we befriended African sailors who met Jesus and then miraculously got jobs on ships without bribes. It changed their lives. Then, we ended up in Amsterdam and waited for provisions for our journey home. God brought one of those sailors to Amsterdam; he found us and gave us what we needed to return home. Moments like these are unexplainable, beyond coincidence. A reminder that The Lord was with us each step of our journey.

CHAPTER 36

UNEXPECTED TURN IN THE ROAD

WHEN WE returned from our year in Europe, we were invited to join the staff at YWAM Concord.

We were settled. Our first responsibility was to staff a School of Evangelism. After the lecture phase, the students and staff headed out for outreach in England. Doug and I were to lead base for the summer.

We had a handful of staff. Our role was to maintain the ministry while the other leaders were on the outreach in Europe. I was pregnant with our third child and struggled with exhaustion from being anemic and from the past eighteen months of travel. But we were settled.

When everyone returned from the outreach, it was an exciting time to hear all the reports. The leaders of the base invited us for a time of sharing, a cup of tea, and catching up.

"We are concerned about some things in your life," they said.

That wasn't the conversation topic we expected. The ministry leaders wanted to discuss some issues in our lives. For three days and many hours of meetings, we talked about their concerns. They brought up things we had said or done that seemed less than loyal or less than humble. I was very diplomatic in those talks until someone mentioned something about failure. I am sure the "failure" comment was not a label or meant to hit as hard as it did. But it revealed something deeper in me, something I had run from all my life.

I fell to the floor and was inconsolable. Doug helped me back to our rooms in the main building, and I fell asleep with these words in my mind: *You are a failure, and now everyone will know.*

I have been involved in bringing correction to others. I know how difficult it is to help people see their blind spots and what is holding them back while also helping them have hope and expect that God will work in their lives. I am sure this was the heart of the leaders, yet I heard a very different message.

They made a final decision that our service on the Concord staff was over, at least for the time being. I felt shame and disillusionment about being disqualified as a missionary.

Our material possessions consisted of an older car and a few suitcases of clothes. Even the furniture in our rooms was borrowed. What did that mean for us as a family? What did it mean for our families, friends, and those who had followed after us in missions?

We prayed about what to do next. The leaders gave us some guidelines. They believed in us and our calling to missions. They asked us NOT to go home to our friends and families. They told us we couldn't stay at the mission base but to find temporary work and housing near enough to maintain the relationship. They expected that God would work on us and bring us back to continue serving in YWAM.

It was a perfect storm for me. I was weak from anemia. We had sold everything but our essentials. We had our car, our clothes, and a few dollars in our bank account. We didn't know anybody apart from the YWAMers, and I was expecting a baby in five months. This crisis was more than I ever imagined as a missionary.

PART FOUR

New Direction
Manchester, New Hampshire

CHAPTER 37

A MAP AND A PRAYER

DOUG FOUND a map of New England. We stood over that map with earnestness, brokenness, and dashed dreams. We could have run home, or we could have submitted to God's work in our lives. Nick, the base director, is still one of our most trusted lifelong friends. There were so many questions about this detour. God is faithful and capable of keeping us even when others can't.

We prayed and looked down at the map. We closed our eyes and pointed to Manchester. Manchester would become our new home. There are many ways that God shows us His plans, and this map prayer only happened once. The important thing was that we looked 100 percent to the Lord to help us in such a vulnerable moment in our lives.

Relocating to Manchester honored the counsel of the YWAM leaders. It was just far enough for us to be on our own, yet close enough to continue a relationship with the base community. This new location was very far from our home in western Pennsylvania.

As we started over, we needed a place to live and a way to support our family. Doug picked up a jobs newspaper and combed the pages, looking for something that would fit his skill set. There seemed to be no options. Then his eyes fell on a Manpower ad for one days work. Laboring for a day with a cleaning company was the only option. The next morning, Doug showed up to begin work with Paul Silva. His job was to clean houses.

On the first morning, Paul handed Doug an Electrolux vacuum and instructed him to clean the downstairs rooms of a large home in Bedford, New Hampshire. Doug hesitated. "I am happy to do this, but I do not know how to even turn this machine on."

For years, Doug's work had been teaching the Bible and sharing the Gospel. Operating a vacuum cleaner was an unfamiliar experience. Yet, in this case, it was God's prescription to change both our lives and our perspective on our calling to missions.

Doug worked hard throughout the day, and Paul invited him for the next day's work.

"What brought you here, Doug?" Paul asked. "You have two girls and a baby on the way? Where will you live? What in the world were you doing before I met you?"

It was a big story to explain.

"We were missionaries," Doug said.

"What is a missionary?"

"We were working with YWAM and spent a year in Europe," Doug explained. "Before that, I was a youth pastor. We took a break to settle down and welcome a new baby into our lives. A missionary tells people about Jesus."

"Wait, what? I cannot believe this. I have been praying to know about Jesus."

Doug had boldly and confidently proclaimed Jesus in the marketplace and on the streets of many countries. Now, he was being asked to tell his new boss, and it felt uncomfortable. Doug shared the salvation story with Paul, and he responded. He had been waiting his whole life for this message. God sent Doug in the weakest, most vulnerable, and most disqualified moment of his life to bring the Good News to him.

His days were filled with cleaning houses and with Paul's unending questions. Questions about the Bible and how he could grow closer to Jesus. Paul helped us find an apartment, and he filled the refrigerator and cupboards with everything we needed.

Our temporary and detoured new life had begun.

Several weeks later, Paul greeted Doug with a serious face in the morning.

"I had a dream, Doug, a spiritual dream," he shared. "God gave me instructions. It has to do with you."

Listening, Doug said, "Yes, go on."

"I am supposed to sell you half of my business." Doug's lack of response did not deter Paul. "You need to own the commercial part of my business," he continued.

Doug explained that he neither had the desire nor the resources to accept the offer before him. "Paul, thank you for considering this, but, my calling is to be a preacher, not a business owner."

Paul persisted every day. With each passing day, Doug felt more compelled to do it.

His requests led us to pray. Was God telling us to do this? Weren't we supposed to return to missions?

We sensed God was speaking to our hearts, "You will be like Joseph, working and providing jobs for others at this time of your life."

The first hurdle was over. We were willing. We did not know how to run a business, and the $15,000 loan to buy the assets and accounts seemed out of our reach.

Paul took us to his bank. The loan officer was on familiar terms with Paul and greeted him.

"You want to buy part of Paul Silva's cleaning business?" The loan officer asked Doug.

"Yes," but the words still didn't come easily.

"What are your assets?"

"Well, sir, I don't have any."

The banker looked puzzled.

"What collateral will you give to secure this loan?"

"I don't know."

The bank officer's warm, welcoming demeanor had turned into a questioning frown. "How much experience do you have in the cleaning business, or any business?" he asked.

"None."

"How long have you been working with Paul?"

"Four weeks."

With each question, Doug understood how ridiculous it was for him to be sitting in the banker's office. He felt embarrassed and very certain they would turn him down.

There was silence in the room. As Doug was preparing to say, "Thank you anyway," Paul spoke up.

"I will put up my house as collateral for this loan," he offered. "Please draw up the contract."

The banker was stunned. Doug was stunned. Paul was smiling and relieved to have advanced the project. Doug owned a business that he didn't know how to run. Our dream of returning to missions was farther away than we ever expected.

Paul gave us a crash course. He instructed me about the basics of running a business, accounting, and paying taxes. Doug learned how to run not only a vacuum but all the tools of the trade. Soon we were up and running.

Doug understood how to relate to business owners and how to fulfill contracts. He had the desire to expand, so he learned how to do marketing. Now, he would need more workers. Silva Commercial Cleaning would employ many YWAMers.

He once stood before thousands to speak and preach. Now, in this new direction, he knelt to clean floors and bathrooms. This chapter was not only a new path, but it was also an apprenticeship for hard work, diligence and business skills. It was a career path that received little honor from others. The Lord saw every moment, and we embraced His Word. Whatever your hand lends itself to, do it with all your might.

God is faithful. Doug learned new skills and employed many others.

The map prayer was a desperate step to find our way during a time of defeat and discouragement. It was a confusing mess on the backside of a tapestry. The other side of the tapestry showed it was God's plan to place us for our life's story in New England and give us the skills and resources that we needed for the journey.

Being kicked out of YWAM, which was our mission, was humiliating. It also meant we had to work through very difficult feelings of rejection and failure. What would people think? But it is God and not people who give credentials for ministry.

There are many examples in the Bible and in church history of leaders needing times of correction and equipping to prepare them for places of trust and influence. It is a hard process. However, God can be trusted to work out his purpose in us to bless others through our lives.

CHAPTER 38

FORGIVENESS

> *THE SPIRIT of the Sovereign LORD is on me, because the LORD has anointed me to proclaim good news to the poor. He has sent me to bind up the brokenhearted, to proclaim freedom for the captives and release from darkness for the prisoners.*
> Isaiah 61:1 NIV

MY FATHER

"Tell me about your father."

That was a loaded request from Pam. I avoided eye contact with her, hoping to change the subject.

It was when my life was on autopilot. Doug worked in our cleaning business, finances were stable, and our children were healthy and happy. Our marriage was strong. Still, I was living in a dark cloud.

One day, I woke up with no desire to leave my bed or interact with the people in my life. Days later, I began to think about dying, and that went on for weeks.

Then it happened. I thought about how I would die if I could make that choice. That terrified me as my quiet thoughts contemplate death. The hardest part was that there seemed to be no reason for it, so there was no way out of it. I told no one. In hiding, the darkness gained power until my fears overpowered the shame that kept me silent.

So, I called Pam. She was a safe person, a pastor's wife, and someone who knew me but was distant enough not to be involved.

"Your father, Deb, let's talk about him," Pam prodded.

I responded, "I am okay with my father. He had a hard life. I had a hard life growing up with him, and I have dealt with it. Thank you very much."

"Tell me more."

I responded with some irritation, "I don't think this applies to how I am feeling." The more I resisted, the more she seemed to sense that this was the key to helping me.

It was a long afternoon of denying and Pam's relentless refocusing on my relationship with my father. Our time ended with a prayer. "Why don't you pray and ask the Lord to help you forgive your father?" She said.

I hesitated.

"Out loud," she added. I tried to form my words. I was trying to avoid the emotion that lay just under the surface of my spoken words. "Why don't you speak forgiveness out loud to him? He isn't here, but this is more for you than for him. You need to hear yourself put words around the hurt, and for you to hear the grace being extended through your own voice." Pam encouraged me.

Those first words came so hard. "Dad, I forgive you for all the anger and the fearful times I spent hiding from you. I forgive you for embarrassing me in our little town, for the times we found you passed out in the yard. For the times you didn't pass out but took your anger through your fists into our kitchen walls, smashing through them with strength that came from your own brokenness. I forgive you for never being there at school meetings and for bringing judgment and criticism."

I spoke forgiveness over the pain that I had tried to suppress for thirty years. So, this is what it feels like to go to the prison in my heart, turn the key, and open the door to freedom. The process was painful, but the outcome was freedom for the first time in my memory—real freedom and relief.

In the next few days, I reflected about how I could live my life and ignore this brokenness caused by hurt and unforgiveness. I devoted a lot of time to thanking God for rescuing me. I held my children closer, knowing their lives would be different because of it.

The phone rang. It was my mom. "Deb, something has happened to your father. I don't know what to make of it, but there seems to be a miracle."

I can't tell you how shocking that moment was for me. My father had been an alcoholic all my life, and even as a young child, I remember the smell of beer whenever he was near me. His angry words would become slurred. Drinking was the main constant in his life. My father used to wake up, have a cup of coffee, a glass of wine, and another glass—most days drinking until he passed out. My mother feared his angry tirades, which caused her two emotional breakdowns. She tried hard to appease him and avoid confrontation over his drinking.

I listened as she explained. "Several days ago, your father came to pick me up from work. I reminded him he was getting low on wine. He said, 'I'm done with drinking; today, I gave my life to Jesus, and He has promised to set me free.'"

Those were the most stunning words I could ever imagine hearing. I was afraid to believe it could be true because I didn't want to be disappointed. But it was true. From that day until he went to be with the Lord twelve years later, he lived for Jesus. He never had another drink, and he never needed one.

He would call me and ask how he could pray for me. He expressed his love for me and my family. That was the most remarkable transformation I have observed in my whole life. I always wondered

172 - A LEGACY OF FAITH

about the timing of it all. Somehow there was a connection between my walking out of a prison of unforgiveness and my father walking out of a prison of alcoholism and darkness into grace.

> *Repent therefore and be converted, that your sins may be blotted out, so that times of refreshing may come from the presence of the Lord.*
> Acts 3:19

Many years after he gave up drinking, I sat with my father in the quiet of his hospital room. He was awaiting an operation that would take away his voice. The doctors explained that removing his larynx would spare his life, but he would need to speak through a special tool. From now on, he would sound like a robot. He didn't ask for anyone but me at that moment. His voice was raspy, and he seemed very nervous.

Cancer is an awful subtractor. It takes away your dreams, your freedom, and your last breath. It reminds us of how yesterday's sins and thoughtless habits, though forgiven, carry mortal consequences.

That was the last time I would hear his natural voice—the tone, inflections, and smoothness. I remembered a song he used to sing to me as a child. He would pull me up on his knees and sing to me. Those memories were so vivid. I tried to memorize the sound of his voice in these last hours.

Who cares for fame or fortune?
Who cares for wealth or gold?
Because I find a fortune
Within my arms, I hold

A tiny turned-up nose
Two cheeks just like a rose
So sweet from head to toes
That little girl of mine

Two arms that hold me tight
Two eyes that shine so bright
Two lips that kiss goodnight
That little girl of mine

No one will ever know
Just what her coming has meant
Because I love her so
She's something heaven has sent
She's all the world to me
She climbs upon my knee
To me, she'll always be
That little girl of mine

And when she lays her head
Upon her pillow, so white
I pray the Lord above
To guide her safe through the night

In dreams, I see her face
And feel her fond embrace
There's no one can replace
That little girl of mine

My life has been so marked by his. Years later, I understood.

My dad realized that even if he had a reprieve now from the disease, he might face it again. The next time, he might not be as fortunate. He wrote letters. He made things right with people and cleared his heart of unsettled accounts. He lived with more purpose and had a kinder, more compassionate place in his heart. My mom grew closer to him, and she was his champion beside him, sharing the uncertainty ahead.

Four years later, a routine checkup brought the dreaded news. The invader, cancer, had returned and had found a home around his corroded artery, squeezing the nerve that told his heart to beat.

Again, I sat with him in the hospital as he waited for a pacemaker to regulate his heartbeat. He spoke through his voice modulator. He talked about being afraid to die. There was fear in his voice. He wasn't sure about his salvation. "Dad, the Bible gives us assurance. I reminded him of his very miraculous salvation and how God had changed his life."

He told me, "There are things you don't know. I can never tell you about my life."

I wondered what that could be. I had watched the demons harass him, driving him to escape through sports or alcohol. Some deep shame was hidden in the loudest argument or his slurred drunken conversation. Something was keeping him bound and afraid—something he felt was not settled and something he could never say.

I left him with a kiss. He handed me the handwritten notes he had penned, complaining about nurses at night who didn't respond kindly to him. I wasn't sure how many days he had left, but I was convinced that God had a hold on his life. He needed to be sure of it.

Back in New Hampshire with my family, I was alone at the sink, washing dishes, praying, and wondering about my father. "What was the secret that was holding him?"

I had a thought, not from my mind, as clear as it was loud. "Your parents weren't married at your conception."

"What?" That had never occurred to me. That one line caused me to stop, and time seemed to stop.

"How could that never have been a subject in my life? I hosted their twenty-fifth-anniversary party."

My hands trembled as I called my Aunt Carol. "I have a question, and I need you to help me. I think God just told me about my parents and my birth."

There was a gasp on the other end of the phone. A long silence. What must have been going through her mind as she formed words to respond to my question? "Please never bring this up to your parents. Out of love for you, they protected you from the pain and shame of this. They spent their lives protecting your heart."

I almost dropped the phone as I sat down. Like a movie on rewind, forty years of my life began rewriting themselves in my mind.

"Oh, that is why...."

I was a sickly child, and after two bouts of pneumonia and spinal meningitis, I lay in the hospital with an oxygen tent over me. And the doctor prepared my mother for a hopeless situation. "I don't expect her to make it through the day." It was a desperate time for my young mom. She knelt on the floor and begged God to spare my life so that she would give me to Him and raise me to know Him.

God heard those prayers, and the morning came with strengthened lungs, a steady heartbeat, a second chance, and a promise.

Now, I understood the behind-the-scenes story, the backdrop of my life. I can't imagine the fear and misplaced guilt that must have flooded her mind. It was in a time when "having to get married" was so shameful.

My mother must have wondered if she was being punished. She must have feared that I would be taken from her because of her sin. My mom surrendered her life to Jesus that day at my bedside. She hid her fears and story for the rest of her life and committed to raising me to know the Lord.

Grandma Guido, my father's mother, took me to church as a child. I remember the singing being so loud that I covered my ears. In church, there was always a time when people gathered around the altar to pray for salvation. The same people each week.

My home was anything but peaceful; my father struggled as a young man. He played baseball. My father drank, and my memories of him were always paired with the smell of beer and cologne.

One night as I fell asleep upstairs, I heard a loud argument going on downstairs. My dad and his mom disagreed about the age of accountability. It was such a strange topic to have a heated argument over.

One of them shouted, "I think it is twenty years because that is when the Israelites were not judged upon entering the Promised Land." The other loudly disagreed, saying children could know right from wrong at eight.

As I listened, I thought, "Well, I am eight, and what if it is eight?" I wanted to know the Lord and be sure my sins were forgiven. Throughout the night, I prayed Jesus would make me His, forgive me, and change me. So began my awareness of God in my life.

I read my Bible—one of those small pocket Bibles. I kept it on my nightstand and read it every night before bed.

My mom was faithful to her word and took me to church. I was a typical kid in Sunday school, memorizing verses and learning Bible songs.

My father was an angry man, robbed of his youthful dreams of becoming a professional baseball player. As a young boy growing up during the Great Depression, they left him at home to fend for himself while his mother worked long hours to provide for their basic needs. He didn't have a dad in the home until he was twelve years old. There was so much shame in being brought into the world without marriage and without a father.

My father never knew his real dad, except for one photo in a scrapbook. A large, brimmed hat overshadowed his face, and his absence overshadowed my father's need for identity, respect, and belonging.

Understanding his brokenness and the shame that he had to carry helped me to have compassion toward him. Our home was filled with anger. There were holes punched in walls, broken treasures, and broken hearts.

I escaped by withdrawing and found school a welcoming place of peace. At seventeen, I was more than ready to head for college.

I would go to my Grandmother Daugherty's house, and she would always warmly welcome me in. Yet, as I looked around her home, there were never any reminders of my life or those of my brothers, mom, or dad. Her house was filled with photos, but not ours. Sometimes people would find out that Grandma Daugherty was my mom's mother. They would express surprise that she had a second daughter. I understood why.

It was a time when unplanned pregnancies were humiliating, and they sent away girls to visit relatives in other cities for nine months.

My grandparents lived on Main Street. They were known in the community, and now they were known for something that brought shame to them. My father carried this all his life.

I realized that the subtle messages that I felt about not belonging were not about my value or being loved. It was the shame of my parents and grandparents. That one moment changed so much for me and gave me so much compassion for my mom and dad.

I never told them I knew. There were times at the end of her life when I wanted to bring it up. But I somehow knew that the knowledge God shared with me was for my healing alone.

My journey of forgiveness opened the door for the deepest healing in my life. It released my father to find his way to salvation. It restored my heart. God used this to help me see that my parents loved me and that they had, even in their weaknesses, given their lives to keep me safe.

CHAPTER 39

ACTIVISTS FOR *LIFE*

BLESSED BE the God and Father of our Lord Jesus Christ, the Father of mercies and God of all comfort, who comforts us in all our tribulation, that we may be able to comfort those who are in any trouble, with the comfort with which we ourselves are comforted by God.
2 Corinthians 1:3-4 BSB

"DEB, I HAVE something on my heart," Doug said. "I constantly think about the pro-life issue. I want to do something about it, but what?" This conversation in 1984 was the birth of a new assignment from the Lord. Doug's burden became God's calling for us to join the pro-life movement.

In 1969, I was a freshman at the California University of Pennsylvania. It was a time of social upheaval and political unrest. The Vietnam War was raging. My campus was a magnet for people who were rebelling against all authority and looking to give "peace a chance." The abortion issue was at the forefront. The Supreme Court later changed the law of the land in 1972, making abortion on demand legal in all states. This was a generation of "free love" that refused to take responsibility for their choices and embraced abortion as freedom from the consequences of their "free love" lifestyles.

Karen was one of the first students I met in Kitt Hall while unpacking my suitcase. She was friendly and beautiful, and she made friends quickly. During those first few days of orientation at California College, now renamed California University, we shared about our lives. Karen had been homecoming queen at her high school.

Our dorm was full of blaring music and girls' chatter. Karen soon found a steady boyfriend who was a member of a campus fraternity. That relationship was rocky at first, but she fell in love with him. During one of the rough days, she went out with Mike, another guy in that same fraternity. He was captivating, and she was flattered to be seen with him. It was a one-night relationship, and then she was back again with her true love.

"Can you keep a secret?" She whispered. Her voice was shaky. Something was wrong. I nodded and leaned forward.

"I am pregnant, and Mike is the father," she whispered. "I don't know what to do. I don't have any money. My parents will be disappointed. I could never tell them. Can you help me?"

I had led a very sheltered life in high school. I am sure there were girls in my school who had a similar crisis, but I never knew about it.

I had thought little about abortion. I hadn't considered if it was a moral choice. Now, my new friend was asking to borrow money from me to have one so she could take care of an inconvenient pregnancy. I sought the Presbyterian pastor from a church a few blocks away from my dorm, and I explained everything to him.

"Don't be concerned about this, Debra," he assured me. "Please help your friend if you can. Just use cash because it is not yet legal; you don't want a paper trail if something happens."

I didn't know what he meant by "if something happens." So, I got cash from my school account, and Karen got out of her problem. I later found that the wounds from this decision haunted her throughout her whole life.

Months later, I found her weeping in her dorm room. "What's wrong?" I asked her.

"I can't stop thinking about what I did and how wrong it was."

During our School of Evangelism in Lausanne in 1980, the Holy Spirit reminded me of Karen and how I helped her. I felt the weight of that decision and the guilt that went with it. When I asked for His mercy, I was aware of the full grace of forgiveness. I have learned that God will take even your most sinful choices and turn them around to bring life to others.

In 1984, the Lord stirred our hearts on this issue. I understood some of the pain and desperation of those struggling with unintended pregnancies. I also then knew what the Bible said: *each child is a gift from God, He made us in his image... formed us in secret in our mother's womb.*

Doug had faced a crisis pregnancy when he was nineteen that ended in a marriage and a divorce. He knew how much suffering came from that in his life.

God was speaking to us. But how should we respond?

We lived in Manchester, New Hampshire, and so I sought all the leaders of the pro-life movement in the state: Right to Life, March for Life, Catholic Charities, Operation Rescue, political leaders and lobbyists. With each meeting, I felt more discouraged. These committed activists were fighting an enormous battle for life, and the battle was scarring them, making them angry, and drawing them into a life of exhaustion. They were mad at everyone: the abortionists, the girls and guys involved, and the politicians, who they felt broke promises and let them down in government. Many were even mad at each other.

We decided that there had to be a different approach, a grace-filled and merciful approach that would let us show the heart of God.

Bringing life-giving hope to those who were in crisis was essential. The question was: who would lead the way?

A friend suggested we contact the Christian Action Council. They were working on two different fronts: one to help with political change and the other to establish "Crisis Pregnancy Centers (CPCs)" that would be a compassionate response to the crisis girls and guys found themselves in.

The volunteers at these centers would listen and provide information, support and compassion. They worked with the girls and guys, providing practical help, resources and temporary homes for some. They also took the girls to appointments and supported them as they worked on relationships that were strained in their homes.

This was our answer. A loving and supportive response to very serious situations would show compassion and grace from the Lord. As we shared our hearts with like-minded friends, we heard many stories of fellow believers who were also affected by unplanned pregnancies. Soon, we had a board of directors who were willing to take some bold steps to bring a center into existence in Manchester. We also gathered a group of women who were touched in this area, many of whom had had crisis pregnancies of their own and some of whom had had abortions.

We were all motivated, prayerful, and aware that we had stepped into uncharted waters. How could we become an organization with a high level of trust and respect when we didn't exist? And how could we exist without financial and volunteer support? Our board took a collective step to do what we could and trust God with the results.

Our first course of action was ordering 30,000 pamphlets from Last Days Ministries called "Children, Things We Throw Away." Then we invited friends to help us distribute them, along with a brief introduction to the Crisis Pregnancy Center, which only existed in our minds. We didn't have a center. We didn't even have a phone number. On that flyer, we put my phone number.

If you need help or think you might be pregnant, we are here for you. Call us today.

That was a bold move.

I asked, "What if someone calls my phone and needs help?" My friend, Annie Campbell, helped me prepare for that possibility. I knew she had volunteered with Catholic charities to respond to girls and do pregnancy tests. I thought she had at least taken a test before. She was on call if I needed her, with a house full of her own children she was homeschooling.

We mapped the city, and together with our new friends, we went from house to house, delivering our packages. I looked at my phone with some anxiety and some hope that we might touch a life. "RING." I was surprised at how nervous I got as I answered. "This is the Manchester Crisis Pregnancy Center. My name is Deb. How can I help you?" I was sure the quiver in my voice would have put the caller off, expecting they would quickly hang up.

"Hello, my name is Crystal. I have an abortion scheduled for later this afternoon. Can my boyfriend and I come to your office?"

"Absolutely. Can you come at two?"

And there it was. We had our first appointment, our first opportunity to respond to a couple in crisis, but there were problems. We didn't have an office. I didn't have a pregnancy test for her and didn't know what to say.

"Annie, can you ask Birthright to give us a pregnancy test, and can you come to my home, um, office to meet with an abortion minded couple in an hour?" I got the words out, and she was on her way with three children and a baby in tow.

I ushered the children upstairs, and Annie was in the kitchen with a baby in her arms, reading the instructions for the pregnancy test.

David and Crystal had so many troublesome problems, and we did our best to give them support. Doug hired David to work in our cleaning business. Crystal needed a place to call home. One of our friends agreed to open their home for her. These homes would later be called "shepherding homes." David and Crystal would get married in a ceremony in the backyard of this beautiful home.

This young couple had felt that there were no options for them except abortion, but in their hearts, they wanted another choice. They wanted a chance for their baby to be born into a loving family, one that would have the support that was needed.

This was the first of tens of thousands of appointments that connected couples in crisis with the practical resources they needed to make life-changing choices. Some would become parents, and some would choose adoption for their babies.

We helped establish the Manchester center with an office, trained workers, and an official phone. Then, a sister center opened in Nashua.

Years later, Laura, a girl I met at Lighthouse, our home group, phoned me. "Deb, can I come over? I know you worked with the Crisis Pregnancy Center, and I am in so much trouble."

"Of course." Laura sat in my living room and told me her story. She was in the middle of a divorce, with a fierce custody battle over her two little girls. Unfortunately, she was pregnant from another relationship. As a very new Christian, she struggled to bring her faith into this tough situation. Would the Lord ask her to lose her daughters?

Her lawyer told her she must abort if she hoped to get custody of the girls. Her husband's lawyer would say she was an unfit mother. It was a tearful evening. Despite pressure from her lawyer and the world's message of convenience, Laura trusted the Lord with her life, unborn baby, and two daughters.

She named the baby "Bri." In the next few years, we lost track of each other, but I never forgot that evening of destiny.

Six years later, I was teaching at Faith Christian Academy (FCA). On the first day of school, I was at the playground monitoring the students as they waited to begin their day. The first day was always a wild one, with kids being dropped off, not knowing the rules or who the teachers were. I was working to keep a safe environment for the children when I felt a small hand tugging on mine. I looked down into the eyes of a beautiful little girl. She was frightened by all the noise and the other children. "Are you okay?" I asked her. "My name is Mrs. Tunney. Don't be afraid." She nodded and moved closer to me.

"It is my first day at school. Thank you. My name is Bri."

A rush of awareness poured over me. I remembered when her mother made a very difficult decision to keep her little baby. I was a part of saving her life, and six years later, somehow, she felt safe holding my hand. She would never know the story behind my holding her hand. I whispered a prayer of thanks, for God had turned one of my darkest days into a beautiful, bright one.

When Romania's revolution freed the nation in 1989, one of the first laws changed was to give women the right to abortion. Doug went two years later, hoping to bring awareness and encourage the church to rise to help respond to this issue the way he had seen the New Hampshire centers serve girls. There was freedom, but the Romanian people were still afraid of the future. The uncertainty caused many to choose abortion.

He spoke in many of the nation's largest churches. Initially, few people acknowledged it was even a concern for the church. "Friends, please look around your church," he pleaded. "Where are the children under three?" That awakened the Body of Christ to this need. Soon there were believers committed to rallying the churches to respond and provide help and support so mothers would have hope for the future and the courage to bring children into the world.

Braunda Butt was the director of the centers in Manchester and Nashua. She helped to train the volunteers and churches in Romania, and we helped to open thirteen centers in the nation.

During one of Doug's trips to help start those centers, I was at a traveling team's basketball practice for my teenage sons. Barb was another mother, well-known in the Goffstown community, and involved in many projects and events. We struck up a friendly conversation while we watched the team do a scrimmage. She remarked Doug was usually the one bringing the boys, and I told her he was on a trip to Romania.

"Oh, Romania, I see. Business?" she asked.

"Well, he is there to help start pregnancy centers," I replied, wondering how she might respond to this. She folded her arms. Her body language gave me a message of disapproval.

"You know that I am pro-choice!" Barb said. It was more of a proclamation than a question. I had no way of knowing what her opinion was, and I did not know how to respond without our casual conversation progressing into an argument.

I shot up an arrow prayer, a desperate request for wisdom. My next thought surprised me. *People with strong opinions about this have had some painful experiences that have affected their perspective.* It was the wisdom I needed.

"Barb, many people with powerful feelings about this have had some pain in their own lives. I know I have. You might have as well." With a nod, she relaxed and changed the subject. We never discussed the issue again, but there was a friendship that started from that humble, honest moment.

I often considered this truth when appealing to those on the other side of an issue. If we can acknowledge the pain in people's lives, it could be the beginning of a conversation that will help us share God's truth and the freedom and forgiveness He can bring.

PART FIVE

Faith Christian Center and Academy
Bedford, New Hampshire

CHAPTER 40

FAITH CHRISTIAN CENTER

PAUL SILVA was faithful to walk alongside us while we learned the ropes of running Silva Commercial Cleaning. Doug learned how to connect with owners and supply top service while maintaining offices. Many skills were added to his life. He planned schedules, hired, and fired workers, kept the cleaning equipment operational, and purchased supplies. He became an on-the-job logistics manager. I had minimal experience with finances and administration. Paying taxes, preparing financial reports, working with accountants, and keeping a budget were all new to me. I had to take an introductory accounting class to help me understand how to keep the books. We were so thankful for Paul's wisdom and for God's grace and blessing.

The business taught us many things and provided financial security for our family. For the first time, we had savings, and we purchased our first home in 1986. Our journey from praying over a map to getting the key to our own home was ordered by the Lord.

During these years, we pioneered the crisis pregnancy centers in Manchester and Nashua and a small group called Lighthouse that met at Norm and Nanette Neveu's home. Doug chaired the March for Way of life and the March for Jesus. I taught school part-time, ran the administration of our business, and at times I jumped in to help with construction cleanup on extensive projects. Faith Christian Center

(FCC) became our home church. Our relationship with Pastor Ken and Marietta grew.

During a service in the fall of 1986, the speaker challenged the congregation. He was sharing about his ministry with political leaders in Washington, DC. "Wherever God calls you, you must obey." Then he went off script, saying, "I feel there are people in business that God is now calling back to full-time ministry."

That was a word to my heart. I turned to Doug. That message was for us. Ron Sloboda, our friend, had been our project manager, and he wanted the opportunity to buy the business. A little while later, Pastor Ken met with us and offered Doug a position at the church. It seemed so smooth, like an open door. The position offered half of our business salary, but we felt we could tighten up our budget and make it work. On December 31, we signed the papers, and Silva Commercial Cleaning had a new owner.

From day one, Doug had a big change. He traded his work clothes in for a suit and tie. He went from making his own schedule to being on the clock. He was one of five pastors and the last one hired, so he got the leftover jobs. It was ministry, but it was not a fit for his heart or his skills.

Our adjustment to a half-salary was also more of a struggle than we expected. We knew God had called us there, but as time went on, we wondered why. After a year in the new position, we were feeling lost, even though we were in ministry.

"Doug, a few elders and I would like to meet with you tomorrow. We have concerns." Pastor Ken's demeanor was that of a boss. We lost the ministry friendship with the struggles of serving on a large staff in a megachurch.

When Doug told me about the meeting, it brought back the YWAM Concord meeting. "Why do they want a meeting?" I asked. "Did we do something wrong? How can this be happening again?"

Even though our lives on the surface seemed okay, we were going around a familiar mountain again. Our family was happy, and our marriage was strong. There was abundant fruit in our ministry. No one could make an accusation of moral compromise. Yet, a different group of leaders in a different ministry setting was trying to address an issue in our lives. This conflict caused enough stress that they were willing to confront it. I was determined to avoid the meeting at all costs.

"Doug, we are having a financial issue at the church, and we have to make some hard choices," Pastor Ken said at the meeting. "Many of our staff will be let go, and since you were the last pastor hired, that, unfortunately, includes you."

Doug was relieved that it seemed to be just business and nothing personal. He assured the leaders that he would be happy to continue with all the ministry responsibilities without pay and work on the side to support our family. His willingness to stay made them go a step farther. "Well, there is more," Pastor Ken added. "There is just some concern about how you are doing your job."

"Doing my job?" Doug wondered aloud. "Ken, you have told me many times that I work harder than three men and that I accomplish more than expected. You recognize God's anointing in my life. What do you have a problem with?"

Pastor Ken seemed confused while trying to answer the question. "All I know is that God wants to do something in your life. We are asking you to lay down ALL the ministry roles. Next week will be your last paycheck. Dr. Sam Brown is a counselor that we trust, and he has agreed to take you on."

When Doug came home, he was defeated. Despite his hard work and faithfulness, his leaders were shutting him out. "I don't know why this is happening again, but I will do what they have required of me," Doug told me when he got back. "I have an appointment this week

194 - A LEGACY OF FAITH

with Dr. Brown. Christmas is a few weeks away, and we must figure out how to survive without a paycheck."

We embraced what the Lord was allowing in our lives, but there were many stressful consequences to deal with. Going from a business income to a pastor's salary and then to no income was sobering. Doug began reading through the employment ads in the Manchester Union Leader. Jordan Marsh was hiring carpet cleaners. He could do that.

When we showed up at church the next Sunday morning, our friends were confused. They asked questions like, "You are not a pastor here now? What do we call you? Why did this happen?" No matter how we tried to avoid answering those questions, they were a constant reminder that something was wrong with us. The failure comment from eight years ago resounded in my spirit.

Then there was the temptation to walk away and split the church by starting our own ministry. We knew that was a possibility, and many people suggested it. "If you start your own church, we will be in the front row on day one." Those comments were ones the leaders considered when they let us go. They realized we had many loyal friends who were influenced by us. Their support could have fueled our ego and spurred us to start our own church.

I wondered if the leaders at YWAM Concord had the same concerns. More than half the staff at the base were there from our home church and were loyal friends of ours. Did our leaders think we were a threat in that way?

Our hearts never entertained such a possibility. We had seen a close-up of the devastating effects of a split church with Rich at the Alliance Chapel. No matter what it meant to us, we would never undermine the work of God for our ego or financial gain. I suspect it surprised Pastor Ken and the elders when we showed up each week in the Sunday morning service as if nothing had happened.

Something had happened that caused a storm in our lives, but we surrendered to God's purpose, trusting in the bigger picture for His glory.

So much of the situation felt like déjà vu: being out on the lawn in Germany, packing our bags in Concord, and now this. We were going through instability and financial insecurity. "What was God trying to tell us?"

We had one constant in those times. The knowledge that God was in charge of our lives and could be trusted.

Christmas was a few weeks away, and our last paycheck paid the mortgage for December. So many times, we saw God provide and rescue us: the waiver for the yellow fever shot on our initial mission trip to Brazil; the dolls in Greece; the money for the train from Germany; a place to live in Amsterdam; Bethany's birthday party; and Lord Adams' finding us in Amsterdam with the money to buy our plane ticket home.

I thought of the Lord's instructions in Joshua 4 after coming through the Jordan River and before entering the Promised Land. He told them to make two memorials: twelve stones in Gilgal so they would remember his provision and faithfulness, and twelve stones to be put in the riverbed. Those would only be detectable in periods of drought when the water flow was low. The message was the same. In the struggle, God is there, and he is faithful. In the miracle times, His glory is seen, and remembering that will give you courage for the times of struggle in the future.

When our children ask, "What do these stones mean?" They would see the evidence of God's work in our lives and own that truth for their lives. This memorial would further be a testimony of God's faithfulness to the nations.

Christmas week came. Each year, we would return to our families in Western Pennsylvania. Our children always enjoyed the holidays with their grandparents. Even with all the changes and travels, Christmas with family and traditions brought them some security and belonging. We had enough money in our bank account for gas to Pittsburgh. We had no money for Christmas presents. So, we packed our suitcases and tried to avoid our children's questions about Christmas presents.

The van was loaded, and we were ready to pull out of our driveway when the phone rang. "We have something to drop off," we heard through the phone. "Will you be home for a few minutes?" The Neveu family showed up five minutes later in two cars full of gifts. We opened gifts with them for more than an hour. There were clothes, toys for the kids, and special gifts. It was the most presents our kids had ever seen. God's provision was clear, even in times of struggle. He was with us, and He could be trusted.

Over the six months, Doug kept his appointments with Dr. Sam Brown. During the first session, Sam laid out a sobering statement. "Doug, I have spoken with the leaders from the church, and I understand some of what they hope will come of our time together. I have counseled many pastors and leaders in similar situations with church relationships. You will again have a ministry. Your willingness to commit to counseling is commendable. You realize the door is shut to any future ministry at Faith Christian. I have never seen that to be a possibility in any situation in my years of counseling. So, please let go of that expectation. You will have a future, but it will be somewhere else."

What a way to begin a conversation! When I heard it, I was relieved. Going back into ministry was the last thing I wanted. In the third week, Sam asked Doug to bring me along. He asked how I was doing.

"Fine, thank you," I replied, but I was far from fine. I just wasn't interested in talking about it.

"Just so you know, I am sure Doug will be back in full-time ministry."

"I am not interested in that kind of future, thank you."

Just showing up on Sunday mornings at FCC was enough of a struggle for me. I had no intention of being back in any kind of ministry.

During the next six months, Doug worked cleaning carpets, and we kept our family together.

One evening, I heard Doug's van pulling into the driveway. He was calling for me when he opened the door. "I finally understand," he said.

For the next few hours, he explained his life to me from a new perspective. This revelation that came after months of talking with Dr. Brown. "My father loved me, but he never told me he loved me. He didn't hug me. He just gave me projects, jobs and responsibilities. He never affirmed me except for completing a task, and that was more of an 'okay, good, here is the next job for you.' I only received my father's approval for working and completing jobs, so I transferred that to my ministry relationships. I worked hard but communicated little. I surprised my leaders and sometimes cut corners to get the job done, but many times, they did not know what I was doing or why. The lack of communication caused a lack of trust and a breakdown of the relationship. I see it now."

Earl Tunney was such a committed father. He was a provider and a kind man, but not an affectionate person. I remember when Doug first gave his life to Jesus, he would tell his dad, "I love you."

"Okay," was the response. Doug started hugging his dad, and it was like hugging a statue. His love language was acts of service, and he served his family well. But the message Doug got was: If you want to be loved, work hard, and deliver a finished project.

"When are you going to get an actual job?" was the often-repeated question from Earl. He seemed disappointed that Doug was a pastor and not in business or some other more recognizable profession.

As his father was well into his eighties, a friend of the family told Doug, "Do you know how proud your father is of you? He brags about you all the time. When you are on a trip, he tells us where you are and what you are doing. He never stops saying how thankful he is for the man you have become."

"So, now what happens?" I asked, wondering how the new insight would help us move on with our lives.

Pastor Ken asked Doug to come in for another conversation. "Dr. Brown has shared with us how things have been going. The elders and I have been amazed at your response to our requests. We half expected you to leave. We wondered if you would start your own ministry. Our respect for you has grown as we have seen your faithfulness, your character, your respect and your willingness to trust the Lord through this time."

Ken then gave Doug a blank piece of paper. "If you could have your dream job, what would it be? What do you love? What are you the best at?" For the next few minutes, Doug wrote:

> I love evangelism and missions. I love training people to share their faith. I love to make a difference in the pro-life area by inspiring people to get involved. I love mobilizing people to reach their communities with the Gospel. I am at my best when I can equip people for the ministry and disciple them in their walk with the Lord.

Pastor Ken read the list and put his signature on the paper. "Welcome back. We would like to have you back on our staff, and this will be your job description."

CHAPTER 41

SCHOOLS OF EVANGELISM AND MINISTRY

PASTOR KEN opened a world of opportunities for Doug. It was a chance to live his dreams and fulfill the calling God had equipped him for. Faith Christian Center had the financial resources and people that could support and launch new initiatives.

His first day back at work was so different. He traded in his suit and tie for more casual attire. He was off the clock and out of the church building. For Doug, that meant he was on God's timetable. If your ministry is in your appointed lane, it hardly feels like work.

The following Sunday, he announced an outreach for the following week. Thirty willing and inspired people showed up with high expectations. Doug took them to the inner city of Manchester. We prayed over the team, and they reached out to people on the street. It was a total flop. They weren't prepared and struggled to engage people in conversation. They got frustrated trying to answer questions, and they met with a ton of rejection.

Despite our encouragement, this experience dampened their enthusiasm. Two people showed up for the next outreach. It was time to rethink the way we were doing outreach.

New Christians find it very easy to reach out to their families and friends. Testimonies are a powerful way to share the Gospel.

Unfortunately, after a short period, they are isolated from those natural relationships. Religious clichés can replace everyday conversations. The gap between Christians and "the lost" grows. It can become a "us and them" situation, where connection and compassion are lost. Evangelism can feel more like a systematic program than an invitation back into a relationship with the Father.

When we talked with some of these discouraged messengers, we noticed several hindrances that held them back.

The most common one was fear: fear of rejection, fear of being misunderstood, and fear of saying the wrong things. We can and must overcome our fears. It is often "False Evidence Appearing Real." Perfect love drives out fear. It is a comfort to know that God is with us as we step out to share with others; He will never leave us.

For some, as they took a step to reach out, thoughts of their inadequacy and failures flooded their minds. How could God use them when they were so imperfect themselves? 1 Timothy 1:5,19 talks about having faith and a good conscience. Accusations from the enemy can be paralyzing. Making sure your heart is right before God is essential to stepping out to serve Him.

Our modern lives are often so fast-paced and centered on ourselves that we lose connection with the needs of others. We need to see people through God's eyes and with His compassion. A prayer like, "Father, break my heart for what breaks yours," will open us up to compassion. Some gave up after that first outreach because they were not connected.

When they were asked questions or sometimes challenged, and they didn't have the answers. It was discouraging.

We realized these issues would continue to hold people back from bringing the Gospel. Evangelists are gifts to the Church to equip her for ministry. This birthed the idea of a School of Evangelism that would prepare believers to reach others with the Gospel.

> *And He Himself gave some to be apostles, some prophets, some evangelists and some pastors and teachers, for the equipping of the saints for the work of ministry, for the edifying of the body of Christ, till we all come to the unity of the faith and of the knowledge of the Son of God, to a perfect man, to the measure of the stature of the fullness of Christ.*
> Ephesians 4:11–13

What should we include in the school?

Our experience in YWAM helped us identify the teaching areas that would be most helpful. The Father, the Heart of God, Intercession, a Clean Heart, the Gospel Message, and Answering Hard Questions were some areas we knew were essential.

Each week, we shared a lesson and gave time for discussion and prayer. After the fourth and eighth weeks, we took the students on local outreaches. There was great enthusiasm. The preparation paid off, and many people responded to the Gospel. The final outreach was a weekend trip to New York City (NYC). It was a cross-cultural experience and a time for trusting God in an even bigger way.

CHAPTER 42

PEOPLE ARE HARD, OR THE HARVEST IS PLENTIFUL

"YOU JUST don't understand how things are here. These people are harder than in other places; they just don't want to hear about Jesus."

We have heard that exact comment on every continent on planet Earth. Often, believers feel discouraged. When challenged with the Great Commission and Jesus' proclamation to *go into the world*, they feel they are the exception to that commission because of the state of the hearts of people in their mission field. Being the exception helps them deal with discouragement.

It has been our experience that there are some places where there is a move of the Holy Spirit and masses of people will respond to the Gospel. In other places, there is a struggle to get an audience to even present the Gospel to one person.

People can appear hard if there is a veil over their minds or if they have no hope. Sometimes they are affected by family or cultural pressures and pride, which cause a barrier to the Gospel.

Yet, Jesus said the *harvest is ripe*. Men and women are lost without Him. God will open doors in the most unlikely and difficult places, where it seems impossible to reach anyone.

CHAPTER 43

LIBERIA

AT THE SAME time, pray also for us, that God may open to us a
door for the word, to declare the mystery of Christ, on account of
which I am in prison, that I may make it clear, which is how I
ought to speak.
Colossians 4:3–4 ESV

KEN WHITTEN, the mission director of our church, Faith Christian
Center, stepped behind the pulpit. "I'm so grateful to be home after
these past weeks in Liberia," he said.

Ken spoke with emotion. "I expected there would be needs in the
nation. I never expected the devastation that this civil war has brought
to these people. It is heartbreaking to see the suffering that these
people endured. I don't have the words to convey the desperation of
this nation. As a church, we must respond and do what we can to help.
We will plan another trip soon."

We knew little about the country. Ken had stirred our hearts, and
we began reading everything available to gain some understanding of
the African nation. The United States founded the nation following
the end of slavery here. Slave ships en route to America and other
nations were turned around and sent back to Africa. They were free.
But it was a humanitarian crisis to bring them back to their homes and

families. They were from different places on the continent. The plan was to begin a new country with all the different tribes.

They drew up a constitution, much like our United States Constitution. They named major cities after American leaders. The nation was filled with factions and tribal infighting. Two great civil wars decimated the nation between 1989 and 1997. Charles Taylor took power in 1997. The two years after were peaceful and then from 1999 to 2003, 50,000 people died. Child soldiers were the main fighters, filled with drugs and the promise of material wealth if they would fight in the revolution. Women brought peace to the nation by banding together to stop the war.

Doug joined the next team to Liberia, along with Pastor Ken and Marietta Anderson. When the plane landed in Monrovia, the team didn't know what to expect. Bishop Reeves and Pastor Sydney Thomas were our key contacts, and they did everything possible to facilitate our team.

The FCC's mission committee had sent forty-foot containers full of medical supplies, provisions, and food. As a result, they were invited to meet with the President. The war had decimated the JFK hospital, and these containers helped restore it back to being a functional hospital.

The team stayed with Judge Ash-Thompson, who was an influential national leader and educator. Doug shared his heart with her to reach people with the Gospel and to train young leaders. Laura Morgan and Doug skipped the meeting with the president and spent their time ministering to a small group of young adults. This group learned the drama, "Doors" and adapted it to their African culture.

Togar Mattias, Alfred Varney, and Francis Klafleh were part of the group. They took on the call to share the Gospel in the future. We later sent bicycles on a container ship. Their drama team would travel from village to village, performing the drama and preaching.

During one of the church services, Doug asked if anyone wanted prayer. He didn't realize that everyone always wanted prayer, and the whole church lined up. He prayed for each person as they passed by him until one young boy caught his eye and his heart.

"What is your name?" he inquired.

"Patrick Whea," the boy answered, surprised at the question.

"Are your parents here?"

"No, I am an orphan. They killed my parents in the war."

"Patrick, God has spoken to my heart; I will be your father. I will call you my son." An African orphan became a part of our family. In the next few years, it was our privilege to support him and help him through school.

CHAPTER 44

MALARIA

WHAT WAS happening? I was awakened from a deep sleep by Doug shaking uncontrollably. He was mumbling. I reached over to calm him, and my hand felt his burning skin. What was wrong? His voice was quivering.

"I am so cold. Get me some blankets." His fever was so high that his body was shivering.

"Can you stand up?" I asked.

I knew I had to get him to the emergency room. Fear was flooding over me. He was not rational. Any mention I made of a hospital visit was met with a resounding refusal. At daybreak, I convinced him to come with me. It was a struggle to get him into the car.

"Watch out, the poles are crashing into our car!" Hallucinations of telephone poles falling in our path were filling his mind.

The admitting nurse in the ER at the Catholic Medical Center ushered us directly into the examination room, and a doctor rushed in. Doug was in a serious state, and they recognized it.

"Have you recently traveled out of the country?" The doctor asked.

Doug could not answer questions, so I answered, "He returned from Liberia four days ago."

They started an IV of fluids, and the doctor went to the outside desk. I could see him with a medical book, skimming through the pages. They did a blood test to look for malaria. It was negative. How could it be negative? Pastor Ken had also been on the trip to Liberia, and the day before, he had fallen ill with malaria with the same symptoms.

"We don't know what this is," the doctor said. "Just rest and drink fluids. We can't give him malaria medication without a positive blood test."

For the next week, he lay in bed with his fever spiking, exhausted. Several times, he attempted to do basic activities. He tried to play with our sons in the backyard and collapsed.

My knowledge of malaria was less than minimal. I was sure my husband was suffering from it, so I read as much as I could about it.

Malaria is a life-threatening disease transmitted through the bite of infected female Anopheles mosquitoes. The malaria parasite attacks and destroys red blood cells, which bring oxygen and nourishment to the body. Every year, over 600,000 people die from the disease, with 95 percent of them in Africa. There are medications to prevent infection. However, the trip organizers did not advise our team to take them. It was a serious error.

When he finally had enough energy to venture out, he went to our local grocery store. It was a relief for him to be out of bed and out of the house.

"Deb, I had a unique experience today. I met a new group of people in the store. I had never noticed them before. The *slow walkers!* I was one of them, leaning on my cart and taking my time as I wandered through the aisles. These were elderly or physically limited people. People I passed by in my hurried life before. But today, I noticed them, and I had compassion for them."

2 Corinthians 1:4 says that we comfort others with the comfort we receive from the Lord. Doug could identify with the physical

limitations of a group of people, and God placed a burden on his heart to reach out to them.

When he returned to the church, he recruited others to help create a ministry for the elderly. Many people who had the heart to reach these people responded, and there was a team that focused on ministering to senior citizens in nursing homes. There was also a special emphasis on accommodating them in church activities.

Doug would relapse and then recover. Then, at random times, he would have another episode. For nine years Doug suffered from this reoccurring sickness. We wondered if he would ever be free from it.

Africa was planted in Doug's heart. The next trip to Africa was planned. It would be a national crusade to bring the factions together, even in this time of war. President Dr. Amos Sawyer asked that the event be named the "Reconciliation Crusade."

CHAPTER 45

RECONCILIATION CRUSADE IN MONROVIA

OUR MISSION group was called Reach Out 2000. We continued to send containers. The Hitchcock Clinic and other medical facilities donated a million dollars worth of life-saving medical supplies. We understood some of the extreme situations that faced the Liberian people. Monrovia, the capital city, had no electricity and no running water. War was sweeping the countryside.

Doug shared the following story of his next trip.

His plane landed on a runway that the war had damaged. There were signs of military presence everywhere.

The team met with Peter Jon de Vos, the United States ambassador. Doug sat at the ornate table with the finest décor. It was impressive. The authority and influence of the ambassador came from the most powerful nation on earth.

God spoke to Doug's heart. *Doug, you are my ambassador. You represent the most powerful kingdom in the universe.* At that moment, he had clarity about his calling to represent the King of Kings, and that position required even greater integrity in his life.

Our team was entrusted with the message of reconciliation for a nation.

> *Now all things are of God, who has reconciled us to Himself*
> *through Jesus Christ, and has given us the ministry of*
> *reconciliation, that is, that God was in Christ reconciling the world*
> *to Himself, not imputing their trespasses to them, and has*
> *committed to us the word of reconciliation. Now then, we are*
> *ambassadors for Christ, as though God were pleading through us:*
> *we implore you on Christ's behalf, be reconciled to God.*
> 2 Corinthians 5:18-20

Our friends, Pastor Sydney Thomas and Bishop Reeves, worked to set up the event. Most of the national Christian leaders committed to helping with the Crusade. Thousands came for leadership and evangelism training.

Doug met with President Sawyer. The meeting was initially scheduled for five minutes, but the President was so engaged in the conversation that it turned into an hour and a half. Dr. Sawyer told Doug that he was having a malaria episode. Doug was experiencing one as well and had to overcome exhaustion every day.

"Rev. Tunney, how should I lead this nation? We are so desperate for a new start."

"Sir, the best counsel I can give you is to read your Bible and do what it says." Dr. Sawyer leaned forward. "Yes. What do you need for this crusade you have planned?"

The president was so committed to helping us. He was so convinced that God was going to use that moment to bring the nation together that he committed all his resources to help us. He gave us the Presidential Palace Hall for the training of 3,300 leaders. The four-day crusade would be held at Antoinette Tubman Stadium. It was an unprecedented event to change a nation and bring forgiveness and restoration.

The crusade training brought together leaders from all major Protestant denominations. The School of Evangelism materials became textbook teaching materials. One session focused on having a clean heart to be used in God's work.

But in a great house there are not only vessels of gold and silver but also of wood and clay, some for honor and some for dishonor. Therefore, if anyone cleanses himself from the latter, he will be a vessel for honor, sanctified and useful for the Master, prepared for every good work.
2 Timothy 2:20–21

Now the purpose of the commandment is to love from a pure heart, from a good conscience, and from sincere faith.
1 Timothy 1:5

.... holding the mystery of the faith with a pure conscience.
1 Timothy 3:9

... having faith and a good conscience, which some having rejected, concerning the faith have suffered shipwreck.
1 Timothy 1:19

The church holds a culture together through its influence on the lives of its people, the integrity of its leaders, and the heart of the family. The prayers of the Saints help guide those in positions of authority with honor and wisdom. When the church is compromised, it loses the impact of righteousness. There is a void, and the enemy will tear apart the fabric of the nation.

Reach Out 2000 took on the responsibility of providing food for those attending the training. Many people walked for days to attend and slept on the ground overnight. After several days of teaching, Doug addressed the foundational message of holiness in the church.

"Are you a Christian?" He asked. He could hear the whispers of "*yes*" throughout the crowd. There were some questioning looks. *Of course, we are!*

"Are you a biblical Christian, or are you a cultural Christian?" He asked again. There was a hush now. He went on, "The Bible says:

Be imitators of God, therefore, as beloved children, and walk in love, just as Christ loved and gave Himself up for us as a fragrant sacrificial offering to God. But among you, as is proper among the saints, there must not be even a hint of sexual immorality, or of any kind of impurity, or of greed. Nor should there be obscenity, foolish talk or crude joking, which are out of character, but rather thanksgiving. For of this you can be sure: No immoral, impure, or greedy person (that is, an idolater), has any inheritance in the kingdom of Christ and of God. Let no one deceive you with empty words, for because of such things, the wrath of God is coming on the sons of disobedience. Therefore, do not be partakers with them."

Ephesians 5:1-7

"You have significant influence if you have a holy life. This nation needs men and women of integrity and holy character if it is to find healing from the destruction that is tearing it apart.

"Who has been living a compromised life—in sexual sin, cheating, lying, or killing? You must repent for your lives to be right with God, and you must repent and help your nation to heal."

The Holy Spirit touched the souls of these leaders, and they cried out, repenting of the sins of their lives and the sins of the nation. For over an hour, the cries continued. The sound was so intense that Doug had to cover his ears. Pastors and leaders were weeping over the most horrendous sins.

Doug was asked many times what contributed to the crisis in Liberia. This was one underlying reason. How can God bless a nation when His Church has compromised in so many ways?

After repentance comes freedom and the joy of the Lord. The Africans danced with joy, and Doug danced with them, celebrating their freedom and deliverance.

When Doug asked the Liberians what would bring in people together in this time of war, the overwhelming answer was a soccer game. The team reached out to several well-known soccer teams, but no one will play for the event. They considered it too dangerous. The blind team from Liberia agreed to play against the lame team. The ball had a bell inside, and men stood beside both goalposts with clacking sticks for the blind team. Many of the players on the lame team were injured in the war. Some were on crutches, and some had to drag themselves in the dirt to get to the ball. They were all skilled athletes and played despite their handicaps.

Our team gathered with the 3,300 leaders in the stadium. The stadium filled up to capacity. There were over 10,000 attendees on each of the four days. The total for the four days was 50,000, and 5,500 people accepted Jesus for the first time. God moved powerfully. The Liberians started hundreds of churches the very next week.

CHAPTER 46

POWER TEAM CRUSADE

THE REACH OUT 2000 crusade in Liberia sparked an idea for Doug. "What would bring people out to hear the Gospel?" was the question he asked before setting up the meeting. The soccer game between the blind and the lame teams was an essential component of the Monrovia event.

If we were to have an evangelism event in Manchester, what type of program would draw a crowd? Pastor Ken suggested John Jacobs and the Power Team. They would hold motivational assemblies in schools, complete with feats of strength, and then invite students to an evening event where the Gospel could be presented.

Taking on such a project was beyond our abilities, so from the beginning, we knew we needed a big team. The many schools of evangelism that we had done in churches all over the state now became the recruiting pool to engage volunteers to help us.

We knew prayer was essential to the success of this event. Prayer was the first thing!. Doug formed a prayer team of pastors who were his friends to support him 24/7. This group became the New Hampshire Pastor Alliance. People prayed, and it set things in motion.

Churches signed up to help with logistics, advertising, and onsite volunteers for the event. Each church committed to taking offerings to support the crusade. We signed a contract for the ice arena. The material list alone was overwhelming. Hundreds of cement blocks and giant ice blocks had to be purchased. The power team would break them as feats of strength. Twelve sets of handcuffs were needed. John Jacobs would snap three sets each night when he talked about the power of God to break the chains of sin.

Over 150 churches were involved, and over 300 people helped us in all these areas. Governor Steve Merrill agreed to attend. Cathy Burnham, a well-known news and entertainment anchor for WMUR television station, would be our mistress of ceremonies.

The Power Team had an excellent program for schools, and eighteen schools signed up for school assemblies. The Catholic diocese joined in with a program at Trinity High School Prisons in Concord, and WMUR televised these school events and made them available to all schools in the state.

We saturated the state with Power Team news.

"Wherever I go, at the water fountain or in our boardroom, people are talking about the upcoming Power Team event," one volunteer said.

It was a move of God. Each day, many small and large miracles happened. There were open doors, donations, connections and open hearts. One phone call comes to mind. We were calling businesses to ask for donations, and our volunteer dialed the wrong number when she was trying to connect with the Coca-Cola distributor in town.

"Hello, is this the Coca-Cola office?"

"No, this is a personal phone. What are you calling for?"

That mistaken call ended with our office person leading them to a commitment to Jesus.

It was a wave, a move of God. The Church (people from many churches united with one purpose) was sharing the gospel, reaching young people, and working together to touch our entire state.

After all the work and prayers, we opened the doors on the first night. Five school assemblies had happened during the day. The motivational messages inspired students. An enormous crowd was already waiting to come in, and by the time the ice arena opened, it was full.

John Jacobs gave a gospel presentation, and hundreds responded to the altar call. Every night, the same thing happened. Over 20,000 people attended the four evening programs, and over 3,000 came forward to receive Jesus.

It was the largest Christian event in the history of New Hampshire, energizing the church and making Jesus famous throughout the land.

CHAPTER 47

ROMANIAN WATER FOUNTAIN MIRACLE

"THE LAMB has won!"

December 16, 1989, was the day the Romanian people took to the streets of Timisoara to resist the communist regime of Nicolae Ceauşescu. For forty-two years, he oppressed the nation with brutal military force. The government rationed food for many months, and now there was no bread. Although farmers had raised the crops, the government exported the product to other nations. The people were starving while Ceauşescu built another mansion for himself.

Piata Victoriei, or Victory Square, is in the center of the city. An elegant fountain is in the middle, with old-world buildings lining the street and the Orthodox cathedral at the edge. That was where the revolution began.

They met the protestors with military force, and many perished. The soldiers killed children and mothers on the steps to the Cathedral. Common people fought back with knives and weapons formed from household items against tanks and machine guns. The soldiers were relatives to the people dying in the streets. Finally, the military refused to attack their people. Victory Square was a sacred place where many gave their lives, hoping for deliverance.

Our Romanian friends recounted the story to us. "When the soldiers laid down their guns, we knew God was on our side and there would be freedom. Many secret disciples of Jesus had prayed for this day for years. They put handwritten banners out of the windows that read, 'The Lamb has won.' Freedom came to our land."

In 1991, Doug went with a team to Timisoara. The social needs confronting the nation moved his heart. The abortion rate was one of the highest in the world, and even though the people were free, there was a lack of hope for the future.

He took a team to Victory Square and shared the Gospel with a crowd that had assembled to watch the Doors drama. Dr. Elizabeth, the director of the Timisoara Pediatric Hospital, met Jesus that day in the streets. She had a genuine encounter with the Lord and became a devoted disciple and a trusted friend. Victory Square was a place of political revolution. More significantly, it was a place where Romanians heard the Gospel.

Doug shared with the church leaders in the city and encouraged them to stand for life, creating crisis pregnancy centers that have flourished till now and brought hope to many families by providing support and practical resources for pregnant mothers.

Several years later, we came back with a team of Joshua Generation youth. We brought medicines and supplies for Dr. Elizabeth's Pediatric Hospital. Our teens took an offering to buy air conditioners for sick infants in the critical care unit.

Local churches provided housing and meals. They told us that the environment was changing, that the government was now "cracking down" on groups in the Square, and that they had been denied permits there. They applied for special permissions in other parks for our team to do outreach. We went to the other parks, but those gathering places were empty.

Doug asked if we could go to the main square. Our hosts replied they were confident police would stop us if we attempted to do anything there. The believers who had experienced a taste of freedom were again living in fear.

"That square is a holy place, friends. That is where your nation began its pursuit of freedom and where many people have come to Christ. We feel called to share the Gospel where crowds gather. I understand your concerns, so we will continue as YWAMers and go alone so you won't get into any trouble with us."

That was a daring step. We gathered up our speakers and headed to the square. Our hosts assured us they would pray, and they thanked us for our understanding. Our red team shirts had a YWAM logo on them, and the twenty-five of us stood out as we walked through the square to the fountain. People stopped and watched, wondering what was about to happen.

Along the way, a Romanian gentleman who was walking through the square stopped us. He was informally dressed in shorts and a tank top. "Hello, YWAMers!" he spoke in English. "It is very nice to meet you here today. My daughter went to a DTS in Egypt several years ago." His friendly smile and manner were reassuring.

My heart was racing. All the cautious warnings were running through my mind. I was taking teenagers into a situation where I could not guarantee their safety.

A crowd gathered as we set up our outdoor speakers. "Good afternoon, ladies and gentlemen. We from America and want to share a message with you through music, dance and a play today." The teens began to do street dance to draw a crowd.

From the four corners of the square, police began moving in our direction. They crowded around Doug, and through our interpreter, they asked for our permit. "You must cease immediately!"

The team continued dancing. The police were emphatically telling Doug to leave.

Then our new friend, who had greeted us a few minutes ago, stepped into the middle of the conversation. He spoke in Romanian. The police listened and nodded. The chief police officer handed him an official-looking logbook. He took a metal seal out of his pocket, stamped the book, and signed it. No one spoke a word. He gave the book back, and all the police dispersed.

"Now, my friends, you are under my authority. Please preach the Gospel."

A huge crowd had gathered because of the commotion, and Doug invited them to accept Jesus as their Savior and to kneel in the street. Over 100 people knelt and started praying after our interpreter. "Father, we come to you today as sinners in need of forgiveness."

Our friend watched with a broad smile of approval as people prayed to give their hearts to The Lord.

"What happened here?" I asked him afterward. "Who are you, and what authority do you have to help us?"

He replied, "This morning, I was in my office in the government building and asked God for His plan for my day. I am the director of the human rights division here. I spent many years in prison for my faith, and now I have an influential position in the government. I sensed God telling me to change my clothes, take a walk through Victory Square, and bring my official seal. Something would happen where I would need it. When I saw your red shirts—a small troop of YWAMers—I realized God had sent me here to help you share Jesus. I am the only person in this city who could have given you the approval to perform here today."

"The Lamb has won!"

Courage isn't the absence of fear; it is stepping out in faith despite fear.

CHAPTER 48

JOSHUA GENERATION

"MY SON isn't walking with the Lord anymore; can you pray for him?" Of course, I would pray, but that request from my brokenhearted friend caused me to stop and wonder about the other young people we knew from our church. Several other parents reached out with similar concerns about their teenagers.

Faith Christian Center was our growing megachurch. There were five pastors and a youth minister. The youth group was filled every week, and retreats and special events happened on a regular schedule. Most of the youth attend Faith Christian Academy, the school founded by our church.

All the extras were available to the young people. On the surface, it seemed like there was a healthy atmosphere for spiritual growth. What was missing?

I was concerned for the families that shared their hearts with us. But I was more concerned that someday I would be the one asking for the same prayer for my own sons. What could I do to help our boys in their faith?

One word I shared with those other parents was, "Guilt and shame over your mistakes will only make it more difficult for you to reach your children. These deep emotions can cause you to withdraw and avoid them or try to control them. Both reactions can push your children farther away from you."

Adam and Eve were placed in a perfect environment with a perfect father, God. There were no bad influences, and every need was met. Yet, the enemy led them both astray when he caused them to distrust the character of God.

When I think of all the mistakes we made as parents including many we were unaware of, it is sobering. Yet, we trust in God's care and love for our families. We do the best we know; we place our children in His hands.

My prayer was, "God, what do these teenagers need?"

"What do you need?" was the thought that came into my mind.

What did I need? I needed an encounter with God, intimacy with Him, and to know Him personally. I needed friends—true believers who would encourage me and walk with me through the difficulties of life; friends who would lift me up and pray for me. I needed a purpose in my life. I wanted to be used by the Lord to reach and serve others and make a difference.

If young people needed what I needed, then I could see how we were missing it with the programs and church events. They were spectators. They needed to get into the game and experience true faith for themselves.

Seeing a need is not always a call, but for me, this was a call to action. It was about my sons. I shared my idea for a summer outreach with other parents. We could bring a team of young people together and let them experience God's touch, worship, make friends, and go on outreach with the Gospel.

Fifteen teens, friends of my sons, had stepped up to be a part of the first group, the experiment. A friend of a friend designed the logo for the shirts. Another mom created a few dances, never mind that most of these teens were unaccustomed to dancing. They learned the drama "Doors."

We spent a week training them and then a week on the outreach. We planned a fun day at an amusement park in the middle of our outreach. That was why Sean showed up. Several weeks before, he had prayed to begin his life as a believer. He had never read the Bible. His family had just taken the first step by coming to church. He was on the baseball team with our sons.

Doug opened the week by talking about having quiet times and listening for God's voice. He sent the group out to seek the Lord and wait in His presence. When they returned, we heard many of them talk about God being real to them for the first time. They asked for prayer for healing and for other things in their lives. Forgiveness was given for many wrongs. They were encountering God.

Pastor Mason, from Wellsville, New York, agreed to host our team for an outreach. He received us and led us in a time of worship. Then he told us to be aware of the enemy. It was a quiet suburb, but Pastor Mason warned us that there was much spiritual warfare.

Watch out for the devil!

After that terrifying introduction to the outreach, more than a few of the teens were ready to have their parents pick them up. One of the college-age leaders had to be coaxed back from taking the first bus back to Manchester. Pastor Mason's goal was to make the troupe of young people focus and realize it was serious business bringing their Gospel show to town, but he instilled some fear in most of us.

The next morning began with quiet time. Afterward, Sean spoke up.

"Can I share something important?"

"Absolutely," I assured him however, I was concerned about what he had to say.

"I had a dream from God, and it is serious."

How do you respond to that? It is the same when someone says, "God spoke to me to do this." If you question it, you go against God or question the integrity of the person. If you go along with their divine revelation, you do not know where it might lead or what consequences will result.

Fifteen teenagers instantly got silent and leaned in to hear about his dream. After Mason had instilled the fear of God in them, it was obvious they were ready to hear the revelation.

"I dreamed about a gas station."

Safe enough.

"And it was a Quick Fill gas station."

No worries.

"And the word *death* was written over the gas station."

That was when a collective gasp came through the room. What could that mean?

My take was that Sean had an overactive imagination. I pretended that what had just happened hadn't happened. I changed the subject and hoped that when the lights were turned off at night, we wouldn't have fifteen teens all having weird dreams of their own.

We were ready to go out for our first street outreach, equipped with two hip-hop dances that non-hip-hop dancers would perform. There was a ton of enthusiasm but not much rhythm. The drama was ready. Everyone had a wordless book to share the Gospel.

The first stop was to fill the vans with gas. There it was: the gas station in Sean's dream. As the young people read the gas station sign when we were pulling in, there was a nervous and excited reaction.

Quick Fill... What? Sean's dream?

Before we could tell them to stay in the van, they were already pouring out, talking fast, and trying to put together the clues of the dream. The attendant was pumping gas.

"Say, Mr. Gas Station Guy, we are Joshua Generation," Sean proclaimed. "What's your name?"

"Lucky!" the startled attendant replied.

"Hey, I had a dream. I saw this gas station and the word 'death' written over it."

At that moment, Lucky stopped pumping gas. "What? Well..." His voice was shaking, and tears rolled from his eyes with every blink. "My wife died five years ago, and my heart has been broken."

That was the young people's signal to jump into action.

"Lucky, can we pray for you?" Immediately, Lucky nodded, and fifteen pairs of hands reached out to bring prayer and hope to the broken man.

"Lord, please touch Lucky. You sent us here to tell him You love him."

He was sobbing, and all the teens were joining in with tears of their own. "God is going to heal you," they said.

Doug asked him if he knew where we could set up to do a show the next night. Across the street was a bar with a parking lot. Doug asked the owner if we could have a community gathering there. Yes. Lucky helped us set up chairs and sat right in the front row. He had invited all the customers who came to his gas station for the day, and the parking lot was full.

After the drama, Doug invited the crowd to receive Jesus. Lucky was the first to raise his hand and pray with the young people.

The outreach yielded its first fruits. It was a model for subsequent youth missions. The youth gained intimacy with God and great friends and were activated for service.

CHAPTER 49

INTIMACY WITH GOD

THE FOYER of our church was full of sleeping bags and suitcases. Thirty teenagers were hanging out, waiting for the church service to be over so they could leave with Joshua Generation for Atlanta, Georgia. We would meet up with 9,000 teens from around the world at a YWAM gathering called Target World right before an outreach at the 1996 Olympics.

Despite the ushers shushing them, they were very loud. Who could blame them? The anticipation for the trip had been building for months.

The trip had a personal meaning for us. Before the outreach in Atlanta, we would spend a week in Concord, New Hampshire, in the facility where we began our missionary journey seventeen years ago.

That time we spent at the YWAM base in 1979 changed our lives. The property was later owned by a local church. Anticipating the drive on Mountain Road already brought back a fresh rush of vivid memories. I remembered God drawing us closer, deeper into the Bible, and deeper into knowing Him.

In our Discipleship Training School in 1979, Ramona Mush, one of our teachers, spoke to us about intimacy with the Lord. She challenged us to seek God, not for what we could get from Him, but to know and love Him with all of our hearts.

Ramona's message challenged Doug and inspired him to seek the Lord in a new way. He shared his experience with me.

CHAPTER 50

SHOES – SIZE 11 WIDE

FROM THE first day I shared the Word of God, I preached on falling in love with Jesus. I was driven by my commitment to love God and encourage others to do so, yet what Ramona taught was different. It was more of an invitation to friendship and fellowship.

After the meeting, I went to the vast field behind the YWAM center, and it ended up becoming a sort of outside chapel.

New England is stunning right now. Today was a most beautiful day; the sky was deep blue, and the trees were like a pallet of paint in an artist's hand. As I ran into the field, the crisp air blew into my face.

God's presence was there. It was holy ground. I burst into song and dance, worshiping with all my heart. And then it was as if the sky opened, and I could see a heavenly beauty overshadowing the fall colors. Another world unfolded in front of me, filled with plants and trees. There were colors I had never seen before. They were translucent, vivid, and beautiful. I knew I saw a glimpse of heaven. I was standing on holy ground, and God was there with me.

It was so unbelievable to me. A thought came to me that caused me to freeze. Wait until you see what heaven is like. It would be more beautiful than autumn in New Hampshire, more beautiful than my wildest imagination, and more stunning than I could ever envision with my natural eyes.

I was speechless. I stood still in God's presence. "Doug, you are amazed at this beauty," I heard. "Wait until you see all I have for you in heaven!"

I heard the Lord ask me, "What do you want, son?" I translated this question into "What do you need?" Learning to ask God for desires rather than physical needs hadn't occurred to me yet.

I looked down at my feet. My shoes were worn and torn, and my socks were sticking out. "Lord, I need shoes," I prayed.

Solomon once asked for wisdom in response to a question like this. Asking for shoes showed how young I was in the Lord and how much I had yet to learn about God's provision in my life.

But seek first the kingdom of God and His righteousness, and all these things shall be added to you.
Matthew 6:33

I know the plans I have for you... You will seek Me and find Me when you search for Me with all your heart. I will be found by you, declares the LORD." What we should want and what we truly need is what God offers: the knowledge of the Holy One.
Jeremiah 29:11-13

As soon as the shoe request came out of my mouth, I realized how shallow it was. I struggled to put together an apology. What was happening in the field that day?

I pondered this as I returned to the ministry building. It all seemed like a dream or a product of my wild imagination. As I walked down the long hall past the dorm rooms, another student called my name. He was holding a box in his hand.

"Doug, I have something for you," he said. "I have been looking for you. While having my quiet time, I had the strongest thought that I should give this to you. These are running shoes. I bought them for myself and have not worn them yet. I hope they fit. Of course, they must fit," he said, smiling. "God knows your size! Eleven wide, right?"

As I held that shoe box in my hands, I realized God had heard my prayer in the field.

It was shocking, but it was much more than getting new shoes. That gift resulted from a new way of seeking God. It was all about an intimate relationship and a personal encounter. What I saw in that field was real. God would answer my simplest prayers, even if they seemed less than noble.

Jesus cared for me and was responding to my love for Him. He had invited me on an adventure that would now define my life.

Each time I laced those shoes, it reminded me that my calling and His provision for me always grew out of my friendship with Him.

I wondered if I would ever tell anyone about what happened in that field because I wasn't sure what happened. Shaking my head, I mumbled, "I asked for shoes."

I am not sure what was more shocking: getting new shoes a few minutes after I prayed because I needed them or realizing that God spoke to me. The encounter I had in the field was real, and it was a window into eternity. And even my shallow request for shoes was the request a Father would expect from a son, and He loved to meet that need.

This wasn't the only time God answered my prayers about shoes.

I grew up in Brownsville, a small town, upstream from Pittsburgh, Pennsylvania. The older boys in my neighborhood were bullies and often grabbed and beat me. It was a rite of passage. We were poor, and my parents had little money. My clothes and even my shoes were hand-me-downs from older cousins in the family.

"Lord, please help me find my shoe!"

I had my first pair of new shoes when I was twelve years old. I had a pair of shoes that were all mine. I felt so proud and grateful. Walking through the neighborhood one day, the older boys grabbed me and tossed me around. They shot me with a BB gun. I was terrified and broke loose and ran. I found myself in a field with grass that was over my head.

When I stopped running, I caught my breath. I looked down to see my shoeless foot. I had lost one of my new shoes somewhere during my escape. I felt so sad, having lost something very special. This was my first memory of praying, asking for God's help in my life. "Please, God, help me find my shoe." As I walked through the field, it seemed like I was being drawn in a specific direction, and there it was: my shoe. This was the first time I knew that God was real and that He would respond to my prayers.

(Back to that morning in 1996)

The worship service started. In the foyer, the teenagers were so loud they were competing with the service. My neighbor, Karyl Cohen, caught my eye in the front row. She jumped up and left. As the door closed behind me, I wondered what had caused her to leave. I hoped it wasn't a family emergency. Whatever the reason, it was obvious something was up.

The church prayed for our team and sent us out with their blessing. The vans were all packed with luggage and excited young people.

Karyl drove in, parked her car in front of our caravan, and ran over to me. "I am so glad I got back in time, Doug," she said. "God spoke to me during the service, and I had to leave. He said, 'Go buy Doug Tunney the most expensive shoes.' So, these are from Macy's, and they are the most expensive Italian leather shoes in the store. I don't know why, but God said you would know what this means. I hope they fit. I guessed your size, eleven wide."

CHAPTER 51

REJOICE WITH ME

SUMMERS IN Transylvania are brutally hot. The last three weeks of outreach in Romania were much hotter than usual. Our team pushed through and brought the Gospel to the streets, from big city squares to small villages.

We were not only hot; we were exhausted. We were resting at an orphanage built on a hill overlooking the city of Deva. The smell of dinner cooking filled the air. The voices of joyful children filled the yard.

The orphanage director added a beautiful swimming pool to the property. However, the filtering system was not working. The water was murky green, alive with algae and various insects. That didn't seem to bother the orphans. They jumped in and out of it with abundant joy, seeming not to care about the water's condition. We knew it was off-limits if we wanted to avoid contracting germs.

We had one more outreach in the evening. The teenagers had given their all for several weeks, and they were looking at me with eyes longing for home. They already had stories to tell their friends and family. They had an amazing report of hundreds of people who had prayed with them to make Jesus their Savior and Lord. I saw it in them; they had empty tanks and no motivation to finish one more presentation. My tank was empty too.

The team sat down beside the green swimming pool.

I spoke: "There is a novelty and adventure you experience on an evangelistic outreach as you see people respond to the Gospel. Your focus can be on the needs of the people around you or on your own need to give to others. For me, that doesn't help me take one more step to finish this last outreach. I can't do it for them, and I can't even do it for me."

There were many nods and a few sighs coming from the team.

"Jesus shared a beautiful story in Luke 15 that talks about a lost son. He left his family, demanded his inheritance, squandered his fortune, and ended up broken and homeless. We often call this account 'the prodigal son.'

"The power of this story, though, comes through the eyes of the father who watched his son walk away, not knowing what would happen to him and longing for the day he would return. While the lost son sought satisfaction in the world, the father's eyes never left the path to their home. He waited, longing for his son. It will break your heart to see someone you love leave without knowing where they are, what they are doing, or how they are doing.

"This story is so real to us because we had a lost son and our hearts longed for him every day.

"Doug married and divorced in less than a year as a nineteen-year-old. He had a son, Brian. After many legal custody battles, Doug finally won his legal parental rights. Unfortunately, each visit ended up with conflict and hostile cries from his four-year-old son. He would shriek and say things like, 'I hate you; I don't want to see you!'

"Each visit intensified the hostility. The most difficult decision of Doug's life was to let go and not destroy his young son in an unwinnable battle. It was a release of love. His mother remarried, and Doug signed the adoption papers, releasing him to their family.

"For sixteen years, we had no contact. Every summer, we would visit Doug's parents, who lived a few miles from Brian's home. The drives through the town filled our hearts with loneliness. We watched boys playing in the fields and wondered if it was him. What did he like? What did he need? Was he wondering about us? Our children prayed for him each night. They yearned to know their brother, and we yearned to have our son back. If that pain was real for me and my children, I could only imagine what it was like for my husband.

"It was the middle of June, and I sat alone at our home in New Hampshire. The strongest thought came to my mind. *Clean the attic.* It was a sweltering hot day, like this one in Romania. The room was stifling, and dust filled the air as I brought order to the many boxes stored there. Just as I moved a box of old papers, a blue-covered legal document rolled out onto the floor.

"The papers I held in my sweaty hands spoke to my heart. Brian would turn twenty in a few weeks. I knew it was time to reach out to him. We had honored his other family and had not caused trouble over the years. That was the time to open the door to a restored relationship.

"I took the dusty papers and sat down in the quiet living room and wrote a letter. *Dear Brian,* I started to write. So much emotion came through my pen that afternoon; pent-up feelings and hope flooded my heart. I tucked that note away in my nightstand drawer with a prayer that God would make a way to send it to him. All our earlier attempts to contact him were rebuffed, so it was a leap of faith to hope he might someday read the words I had penned.

"Two days later, we were away on a family day with our other four children. On the ride home, I took a chance and announced to the family, 'It is time we try to reach out to Brian. We should all write letters, send photos, and see if we can find him.'

"The children were wild with expectation. They talked about what they wanted to say and which photos they could send to their brother. Doug sat quietly. 'It has been sixteen years since I last saw my son,' he mumbled. 'I can't get my hopes up.' The excited children prevailed, and we wrote a family love letter to a faraway, almost twenty-year-old son.

"The children dragged our photo box into the living room. Doug and I sat down in our bedroom. With his pen and paper in hand, he began a letter that would carry sixteen years of longing and love. *Dear Brian*, he wrote, and just at that moment, the phone rang.

'Doug,' his brother Randy sounded upset. 'I have very serious and bad news for you. Your son, Brian, has been in a terrible motorcycle accident. He is in the ICU and has severe injuries. I am not sure he is alive since this report is a few days old.'

"Tears ran down Doug's face. His hands trembled as he clutched the pen and paper.

"Just when we made a step toward finding our son, we heard he may be lost forever. Then faith welled up in my heart. I opened my drawer and showed Doug the letter I had written days before, maybe on the day of the accident. God was involved in that crisis moment. What seemed like a tragedy was His opportunity."

As I retold that moment, I fought back tears of my own. I knew the power of a father's love, and I prayed the young people listening around the murky green pool would get a glimpse into God's heart.

"We called the hospital and found that though his injuries were very serious, he was recovering and was released from the ICU. We prepared our love letter, complete with family photos that told our story. Every word was filled with hope for a moment when we would see him.

"Our letter offered an invitation for Brian to meet when we would visit Doug's parents' home in a few weeks. We sent it as a special delivery to his hospital room and waited for a response, any response at all, but there was nothing. Silence.

"Many times, in those sixteen years of separation, we suffered from this broken connection, but our feelings had to be put aside. Our vulnerable hearts were out in the open. We arrived at Doug's parents' home with a fading hope that we would get to meet our son.

"Later that week, I went shopping for the afternoon with our daughters. After several hours, I pulled into the driveway. I heard shouts from our two young sons. They screamed, 'We found him!'

"They smacked the van as they ran alongside, jumping, laughing, and crying out, 'He is here. Our brother is here.'

"A moment later, I saw him. He stood beside his father. It seemed to have always been that way. There were tears for all of us. Brian looked so much like Doug. He walked like him. He even wore the same shoes.

"An hour before, Doug answered his parents' phone: 'Dad, this is Brian. I am down by the traffic light in Rosco, and I am waiting for you. Can you pick me up?' That ride was full of hope and joy.

"Our hearts were filled with rejoicing deeper than words. We found our son. A lost brother was home! This moment was more intense because of our children's love for their dad. I could understand the father in Luke 15 when he calls for gifts and a feast as he runs with tears to embrace his lost son.

"The older brother in this story couldn't share in the joy. He burned with anger, and he felt unappreciated and overlooked. He did all the right things at the house but missed his brokenhearted father's yearning. In fact, if this brother had understood his father, he would have gone after his lost brother and returned only with him."

I looked around at our team and continued, "We can share the Gospel out of obligation, routine, or responsibility. Or we can share

Jesus with lost sons and daughters because we understand our father's heart and how He longs to be restored to them."

"Tonight, we will walk to the town center and do our last outreach. You might not have the strength or desire to give yourself to it unless you look at these people as loved by your heavenly Father and realize that His love is to reach them through your words and touch. If you see them through His eyes, you will share in the rejoicing and understand that it is for Him you serve here."

A quietness settled over our team. We all got a glimpse into our loving Father's heart. Soon, we walked into the town square, and that evening, there was a holiness to our outreach. There was nothing to prove; there was no need for another story to tell back home. We shared out of our weakness and tiredness and because of our love for our Father. It changed all of us so that we could serve with our eyes toward heaven, seeing people through the eyes of love.

"Rejoice with me!" is the theme of Luke 15: the shepherd finds the lost sheep, the woman finds her lost coin, and a father runs to embrace his lost son.

Evangelism can be a weighty responsibility unless it is a response to God's love that compels us to live out that seeking all our days. When we find lost sons and daughters, we join in the welcoming party with Jesus.

"Rejoice with me!" is God's invitation to enter His joy when people are restored to a relationship with him. It is the reason we bring the Good News to a lost world. We continue when our human resources are used up, and there is little glory in the work. Our Father in heaven is longing for lost sons and daughters to return, and we will tell them He is waiting.

CHAPTER 52

THANKSGIVING DAY IN LIBERIA

DOUG'S FREQUENT trips to Liberia were often in dangerous settings. The civil war continued, hampering the relief efforts of our Reachout 2000 teams. Faith Christian Center continued to send food and donate medical supplies. We often heard that the gifts sustained the lives of thousands of displaced Liberian families. Doug felt a sense of urgency to continue these trips, even when many expressed concerns for his safety, including me. This is his story of God's amazing guidance, protection, and provision in Liberia.

CHAPTER 53

CHECKPOINT 13

"WHO ARE you guys? Everybody, get out of the car."

Several battle-ready AFL (Armed Forces of Liberia) halted our cars. They were yelling as they rushed toward us. There was an iron gate across the road at the Owens Grove Checkpoint. We slowed, stopped, and held our breaths.

Our team from Faith Christian Center was determined to make our way to Buchanan, Grand Bassa County, to share the Gospel on November 2, Thanksgiving Day in Liberia. The country was in the midst of a devastating civil war that caused much suffering, misery, and neglect.

My African friends had shared many stories of unimaginable barbarism that they had witnessed. Everyone had a story that would break your heart if you heard it. Everyone lost a close family member.

Our mission with Reachout 2000 was to host a national salvation and healing crusade. Sydney Thomas, a national ministry leader, was the secretary of the steering committee for the Christian Community of Liberia.

"Doug, our needs are so great. Charles Taylor's insurgent fighters are advancing through the nation, creating terror in every corner of our lives. Our people do not have food. They are starving for bread, and they are starving for the Word of God. Your team is the only one to come these days." Sydney's words revealed the burden he carried for his people, who were ravaged by war.

"If we are to share the Gospel in Buchanan, we must leave very early. The curfew has no exceptions. No one is to be out on the roads after sundown. No one. ECOMOG soldiers from various countries man checkpoints along the road to Buchanan. They have orders to shoot anyone breaking the curfew."

I am not a man who reacts in fear to many situations, but his warning made me tremble. "Okay, then. How long will it take us to make this trip?"

"The drive should have taken one hour but will take at least five because of the many checkpoints, potholes, and washed-out parts of the road. Let's leave at 8:00 A.M."

I acknowledged. I thanked God for His peace that passes our understanding. I understood the danger that awaited us in the morning.

"Get out of the car, NOW!"

Sydney had warned us there would be stops like this. Everyone got out of our cars. They would search our vehicles. We complied with every order without speaking, but all our hearts were racing. It did not seem like a routine stop.

Sydney was our driver, and he responded to their questions. "We are missionaries!" None of us was sure if that proclamation would open the door to more trouble or help us through. The soldiers demanded our identification. We observed twenty bodyguards moving our way as they searched through our passports. The Commanding General had been staring from a distance in a makeshift post.

The commander seemed anxious; he now took over the interrogation. "Are you missionaries? Are any of you preachers? Where are you traveling?"

Sydney again responded, "Yes, they are missionaries who have come from the United States to preach the Gospel to our people. We are going to Buchanan for a crusade."

Upon hearing that, he breathed heavily and declared, "This is an answer to prayer! This is a miracle."

We all breathed out a sigh of relief. My heart was still beating with an overload of adrenaline.

The General revealed that when he got up that Thanksgiving Day morning, he prayed to God to send someone who would preach to his men on Thanksgiving Day. He thought his men had been in the bush fighting the entire year and should take a break for at least an hour on Thanksgiving to thank God for sparing their lives. "Lord, who will speak to my men?" he prayed. God spoke to his heart, "I will provide a preacher." He had been waiting for us.

He looked straight at us and added, "I recognize your journey is far ahead of you, and the road is rough, but if you do not mind, could you please take some time to preach to my men?"

I nodded. "We are delighted at the opportunity to preach to your men."

The General commanded the men to come to the Baptist Church across the road. It was a building marked by war. Half the side wall had been blown out with a rocket, and there were bullet holes scattered throughout. From their bunkers and holes, four hundred men appeared out of the bushes. They were dirty and dusty, and carrying their armaments. They all carried weapons, ready for any unpredictable trouble.

Dick Aucoin preached the Gospel. The Lord laid on my heart a message for the moment about murder and killing in war. "In battle, you may take another life to protect yourself or innocent people, but many men in war become murderers, are full of hatred, and kill innocent people. Are you guilty of this?"

I motioned toward the General. He was the first to respond to the altar call, surrender his life, and ask for forgiveness. He moved forward and knelt at the altar. Almost all the men followed him, equipped for battle, and were now yielding to the Lord, who could forgive them of any horrible sin.

We continued to Buchanan and did an outreach throughout the afternoon, with hundreds responding to the Gospel. As we began the trip back through many checkpoints, our Liberian friends were anxious. We shared the song "Checkpoint, check your heart!" and gave the soldiers food along the way. As we traveled back to Monrovia, they recognized us and passed us through without stopping to make it back before dusk.

On the return trip, Peter, a director with Every Home for Christ, was with me. I told him this story, and he questioned it. "That is unbelievable. I am not certain I trust this story."

We stopped in front of the Baptist church and got out of our car. "Here is the place, Pete. God did an amazing thing here. After Thanksgiving Day, we sent Bibles to be distributed to the soldiers."

Just then, a woman who was in the market nearby recognized me. "Hey, you are the man of God that brought the Gospel to the soldiers here. Those men would come here every day to pray. I am now the pastor of this church and have been ministering to them."

Peter nodded. "What an amazing God we have."

As word spread throughout the nation, Checkpoint 13 became a symbol to the soldiers that God saw them in the crisis of war and sent a messenger of God to share the Gospel. When I was in South Africa several years later, I heard this story. This is known throughout Africa as a testimony of God's provision and heart to bring the Gospel.

CHAPTER 54

MEGAN

"I WILL BE your sons' coach again," Dan Lynch said when he phoned me. "Do you remember Megan from the team last spring? Her dad just called and said she has cancer. We want to have a fundraiser to help with the cost of her treatment for lymphoma. It is a tough time for her family. Can you help us host a bake sale?"

Of course, we knew Megan. She was a thirteen-year-old girl holding her own against a team of boys in a minor league. Most girls drop out of baseball in that age group, but she would not be intimidated by the guys. She was an outstanding player, and she was confident in holding her own on the team. She was also an exceptional basketball player.

The coach explained that her family had lost health insurance and that the bill for each round of medicine would be thousands of dollars. My first thought was that a bake sale wouldn't make a dent in the financial need she had.

We had experience raising funds for the CPC ministry, and I thought a walkathon could help bring in more funds for her treatment. Many friends from the Faith Christian Center, our church, lived in the Goffstown community, and I was sure they would step up and help us with the fundraiser.

Local businesses donated prizes to the players who raised the most money. It was an added incentive, but the players were highly motivated to help Megan with no mention of prizes. The walk would start at the school and end at the baseball fields on Opening Day.

Opening Day was always a community event. Parents and grandparents would fill the stands to cheer on their team. The youth sported their new colorful uniforms and hats. That year had a significant meaning for us all. We were standing by Megan for her life.

I was thankful for the opportunity to connect with the other parents. It had been a challenge to break into the community. New Englanders make friends slowly. We were at every game and practice the previous year but were not included in the conversations held by parents in the stands. They acknowledged us, but we also got the message that we were the new family and not yet accepted into the community clique.

It was different when we were preparing for the walkathon. All hands were on deck to help Megan. I wondered what the Lord had planned for that time.

Megan had already started her treatments, and I was overjoyed that she was strong enough to join us on the field. She was frail and needed help to walk. A bandana covered her balding head, but her spunky personality still shone through. She sat with us, watching the colorful players pour into the field at the finish of the walk. They were there for her.

Doug reached out to Ed, the Little League president. "We have a check for $12,000 for Megan. When we give it to her, I wonder if we, as a community, could pray for her. The money will help with her treatments, but only God can touch her and bring healing."

Ed fumbled over his words for a few seconds. "Yes, um, sure, you can pray."

There were 600 Little Leaguers and hundreds of parents and grandparents, all waiting in anticipation to hear the report. Megan walked over to receive the check.

"We are so grateful for your participation in the walkathon," Doug announced. "We have a $12,000 check for Megan. Would you all join me as we ask God to bring healing and to give the doctors wisdom as they treat her?"

The players bowed their heads, removing their ball caps. No one spoke a word. It seemed everyone knew it was a holy moment.

"Lord, we ask you today for your help. As a community, we pray for Megan that you will bring healing to her for a full recovery and that you will supply every need, including every financial need."

Ed was crying. He was a gruff guy, not prone to showing his emotions, but he was deeply moved. You could hear sobs throughout the field. It was a God encounter we would never forget.

Megan had a miraculous recovery, and in the next season, she was the MVP of the girls' basketball league.

We were known in the community after that time. Many people would stop us in the grocery store or at the gas station and remark about that moment. "We felt so proud of our community for doing something positive. Thank you for stepping out."

Two years later, I was working as an administrative assistant at Faith Christian Center. We had an evangelistic event the previous night, and I was sending follow-up letters to those who responded to the invitation: Joe Smith and Mary Jones. I reached for the next response card...Megan!

I stared at the card, and the events of Little League Opening Day flashed through my mind. God answered our prayers for her life and for her eternal life.

CHAPTER 55

UBATUBA

"TOMORROW WE will leave early in the morning for Ubatuba. The three-hour trip through the mountains is breathtaking. Let's pray for safety on the road."

I was already feeling anxious about the trip, remembering the previous four times we had ventured to the picturesque beach town south of Sao Paulo. On our first mission trip to Brazil in 1974, our time in Ubatuba was memorable because of the amazing response to the Gospel. It was also memorable because of the terrifying drive down the mountain. The bends in the road were so sharp that only the most skilled bus drivers could navigate them safely. There were many unpaved stretches of road and no guardrails along the way. When I asked our Brazilian translators about the many crosses that lined the edges of the road, their response added to my concern.

"Oh, that is where a car or bus skidded over the edge," they answered. "Sometimes it is impossible to retrieve them, so they add them as a memorial."

I was the last person on the bus in the morning. The front seat had a curtain that could be drawn to block the view of the road. That was my seat choice. The bus creaked, making sharp turns. Some items fell from the overhead storage spaces. When we arrived safely at the bottom, I breathed a sigh of relief. Every one of the four previous outreaches to the tourist city had been amazing, and we were all expecting that would be the best part of our mission trip.

As we drove through the village, something was strange. July was school vacation time, and the streets were usually filled with tourists, but they were too quiet. Our host, Pastor Paulo, explained that there had been a school strike, and the schools were in session instead of the usual break.

That afternoon, we went to the beach to share, but the beach was empty. The few people seemed strangely uninterested in talking with us. Our group of twenty-eight from the Lighthouse home group had been looking forward to that week since we first talked about a trip to Brazil.

"What if we can't find people to share with?" was the question we heard over and over.

"Lord, what are we going to do?" was our prayer. Pastor Paulo was apologetic, but he had no alternative plans for the week.

"Let's get dressed for the Doors drama. We will figure out what to do." Doug seemed to have a knack for on-the-spot direction in moments like that. *Pray as you go!*

With costumes on, the team roamed through the empty streets.

"Isn't that a school?" Doug asked, picking up the pace. "Let's see if we can do a show there."

Rick and Liz, the key actors in the drama, accompanied Doug into the school office.

"We are actors from America, and we want to present a play," Doug announced to a surprised principal. She asked how many could see it at one time.

"Four hundred," Doug replied, picking a random number.

The principal said that was how many students they had! We went in, and they called the students out of the classrooms. We presented Doors. Before Doug could give the invitation to accept Christ, the principal came forward, and our hearts started sinking, thinking she was going to shut us down. On the contrary, she enjoyed our performance. She said two other schools met here as well and asked if we would come back tomorrow for another performance. We could go to the classrooms to discuss "our philosophy of life." We were elated and prepared.

When we headed back the next day, we went into each classroom, presented the students with the gospel (through interpreters) using a tract, and did another performance. The teacher in one class, who was wearing a Sandinista shirt (Communist), grew very verbal and agitated. But the students challenged her on why they should only listen to one viewpoint. Afterward, our small group talked with the students, and they appreciated we were not closed-minded like the teacher. I asked if we could pray for her, and as a group, we did.

That night, a teacher's meeting was held at the school, with hundreds of teachers in attendance. We performed the drama "Doors" again, and then Doug gave a powerful salvation invitation, telling the teachers that they needed to renounce certain sins and inviting them to get on their knees to receive Christ. Nearly every one of the almost two hundred people did!

What makes this story even more amazing and miraculous is that it was never supposed to have happened. The reason there were fewer people on the beaches was that they had extended the school year because of a teacher's strike. We got all the young people at once! The principal, who was in charge, was gone, and it was the assistant principal who had let us in. The teachers and future educators of Brazil were all in one place, because of the strike.

Our hosts couldn't believe we had just walked uninvited into the school. They had been trying to get into the school for ten years! When the principal (who was a Macumba cultist) found out what had happened, she called a meeting to fire the assistant principal.

The assistant principal later told us she left the meeting to gather her thoughts, and that God had spoken to her in the bathroom, saying he would protect her. The agenda at the meeting changed when she returned, and they spared her job. The assistant principal had not even been a Christian! She just saw it, perhaps as a nice cultural exchange. It was a divine appointment, and she was in a position of authority for such a time.

There were about 600 people who gave their lives to Christ between the three events, all because Doug stepped out and let God direct the group. When we prepare and believe in God for impossible things, in a brief period, hundreds, even thousands, can be changed for Christ through the power of the gospel.

CHAPTER 56

CULTURAL KEYS

IN DON RICHARDSON'S book, *Eternity in Their Hearts*, he shows us that in every culture and people group, God has placed in their hearts an awareness of their creator. They might not understand who He is, but like those worshiping the unknown god on Mars Hill, there will be a desire to make a connection. There is a moral code within them all. They might not agree on which of their actions is wrong, but they know when something is done against them.

We've been in many situations where connecting with people and presenting Jesus seemed hopeless at first. Cultural and even language barriers can feel like an enormous wall. The secret is to engage and listen. Come to understand the hearts of those you are trying to reach. There is always a door. Sometimes it takes creativity. The Holy Spirit will work through you to reach them.

We took a team of church friends to Taiwan in 1987. In the meetings leading up to our trip, we had seasoned missionaries help prepare our team. Their comments surprised me.

"Welcome to Taiwan. Please don't be discouraged when no one comes to the Lord. It takes seven years on average to see a conversion." That one comment made our two-week trip seem like it could be a monumental waste of time.

Our group responded with faith, and they were prepared to share Christ. Steve Braun, a seasoned missionary, was with us. He was an experienced street preacher. Despite the seven-year downer, we prayed with faith for fruit from our trip.

When we arrived, our Taiwanese host, Pastor Paul, brought us to an outreach house near the factory section of town. The local church had a wonderful plan to engage with nonbelievers by welcoming them straight from work with food and fellowship. Soon, the room was filled with factory workers. A tiny woman approached me and conversed with me through an interpreter. Miss Min seemed very interested in hearing about Jesus. After a long conversation, I asked if she understood what it meant to follow Jesus and make Him the Lord of her life. Her smiling face became serious, and a look of fear came over her face. "Yes, I do. But I could never trust Jesus; I am terrified of the Buddhas. They would cause disaster to come my way if I did." She then disengaged from me, finished her food, and left.

It sure seemed like a seven-year moment as the evening ended. That had been the experience of most of the team—friendly conversation but closed doors with any mention of Jesus. We could have embraced sightseeing for the rest of the trip or asked the Lord for a key to their hearts. We prayed.

The next day, we took our team to a park, and a large crowd gathered to watch our "Doors" drama performance. Several hundred people watched. When the drama finished, Doug took the microphone. When he said "Hello," *all* the people left! That was the first time we had ever experienced a group running away after a street performance. It was beginning to be discouraging.

We moved to a different area, and the same thing happened. Another sizable crowd watched the drama and then, in a second, dispersed before we could even say hello.

We prayed more. Doug lifted his eyes from praying and looked straight into Steve's face. He wasn't a senior citizen; however, he was balding and had a weathered look that added years to his true age.

"Steve, I have heard that in this culture there is a deep respect for parents and elders. Would you mind if we adopted you as our group elder and invited these people to listen to you as a token of respect for the elderly?"

Steve laughed. Our team smiled and called him Father Steve. Our next outreach began the same as the others. Hundreds of people squeezed together in curiosity to see what was happening. The music played, and the actors in their costumes took their places in the street. "Hello, friends. We are a team from the United States and are so happy to be with you today. Elder Steve here is a great friend. We look up to him with honor as an elder. He will talk to you at the end of our short drama. Please show him the respect due him and listen to his words."

The drama began. The crowd was interested and quietly watched. The music stopped. No one moved. I didn't want to breathe so as not to scare them away. Steve grabbed the mic and shared the Gospel, and many people responded, praying to accept Jesus as their Savior and Lord.

Several days later, I saw Miss Min. Many people gathered in the parks at sunrise before the heat came to exercise, dance, and visit with friends. It surprised her to see me. "God must have sent you here this morning. It is not an accident that I'm meeting you again. I prayed that if He is real, I would have another chance to see you."

I assured her that Jesus would protect her and keep her safe. She gave her life to Jesus that morning and joined Pastor Paul's church. Seven years did not apply. God made a way.

CHAPTER 57

GIRL IN A BOX

EVERY MISSION trip to New York City was an adventure. One weekend in December was memorable. The weather was frigid, and there was a snowstorm. We warned the students ahead of time to dress warmly and expect to deal with the weather. Trudy, an eighty-year-old grandmother, came along, which was a surprise to us all.

The challenges of homelessness, especially in the winter, are more than most people might know. If you find shelter in a storefront or a makeshift box house, where do you keep food or drinks without them freezing? Where do you find a bathroom in the night?

Our vans pulled up to Battery Park, located right on the water's edge. The wind whipped the falling snow into sheets across the icy walkways. Castle Clinton is a circular sandstone fort built in the early 1800s as the first American immigration station, predating Ellis Island. It is a historical building near the ferry dock for trips to the Statue of Liberty. The massive round building has small insets where homeless people take shelter.

Trudy was adamant about helping, despite the cold weather. She filled her arms with several blankets, some bottled water, and a paper bag of sandwiches. Leaving her cane behind wasn't the best idea, but she was determined, so the two of us held her arms and steadied her as she shuffled. We almost skated across the walkway to the first cardboard door.

"Hello, we are here to bring you some blankets and food. My name is Trudy." There was no answer to our knocks. The only sounds were the wind whipping and our sniffling noses.

"Anyone there?" No response. As we walked away to the next cardboard "home," we heard the scratching sound of cardboard against the bricks. Out from behind the "door" came an open hand. A weak voice from inside called out, "Please, thank you."

Trudy handed the food and blankets to this nameless person sheltering behind the cardboard. We prayed for them, asking for God to make a way for them to find a better life and to hear the Gospel. We had no way to help beyond giving these small things compared to the immense need.

Trudy's insistence on venturing out of the comfort and warmth of the van amazed me. She told us that evening changed her life and filled her with a deeper sense of compassion. It was the same for many of the team members. Apathy melts into compassion when you venture to touch someone's needs. Someone you know could be in that situation. It could be you or someone in your family.

When the "lost" are the objects of our outreach, it can be dehumanizing. Lost people have names and stories. If we are to be God's messengers of love, we must see them as they are. In Mark 24, Jesus touched the eyes of a blind man twice before he was restored and could see everyone clearly.

After Battery Park, we drove to Manhattan, near the United Nations building. On the drive, we noticed what looked like a person sleeping on a bench covered with snow, so still that you could mistake their body for a statue.

Someone on the team questioned, "Is that a person? Do you think they are okay? They seem to be so still. Should we stop?"

Just then, a shivering elderly man sat up and dusted himself off from the several inches of snow. Horns were now honking at us to keep moving. The city doesn't have time for compassion. We moved on but regretted we hadn't inquired with him. Missed opportunities linger with you.

Our vans dropped us off and looked for parking spaces, which were often difficult to find in the city. The storefronts were filled with makeshift box houses. Some were very ingenious in how they were put together, like tiny houses held together with duct tape. It was still freezing, and the snow continued to pour down in giant flakes. There are scenarios where falling snow brings a sort of delight because of its beauty. That night reminded us that people living on the edge miss the beauty amid their struggle with the chill that the blanket of white brings.

I knocked on the so-called "front door" of a cardboard house. The occupant had created a unique place to call home with several rooms. The area was tidy.

"Can I help you?" A beautiful African American girl in her twenties peeked out of her home. She welcomed me with a friendly voice and a broad smile.

"We are Christians and have some things to give you if you can use them." She received the water and sandwiches but already had enough blankets.

"You are from a church? I am not interested in that but thank you for the food. Our food and drinks freeze on the street, and I am often hungry even with a stack of food inside," she explained.

I thanked her for receiving us and then turned to move on.

"Do you have a prayer request?" I inquired.

She shook her head no, then replied, "I have one request. I am looking for my father. Can you pray I will find my real father? I never knew him, never met him, but I've thought about him my entire life.

What does he look like? Why did he leave my mother? I sometimes wonder if he is right here in the city and might walk by me sometime during the day."

As I bowed my head to pray, these words rang through my mind: I am the Father she has been searching for all her life. I am here for her.

When I looked up, she was staring at me, surprised that I wasn't saying anything. "Your heavenly Father loves you, and He wants you to know that you can know Him. You can find Him right now."

The tears ran down her cheeks, mixing with the heavy snowflakes. She began praying, "Father, I have been running from you for so long. Thank you for sending this lady here tonight to remind me you love me. Please forgive me. I am your daughter. I want to live for you."

She shared with me that searching for an absent father had brought bitterness to her heart. She grew up in the church as a little girl. She had been an accountant and lost her job months ago, and it was a short time between the last paycheck and being homeless on the street. Like the shepherd who goes after that one lost sheep, the Father sent us through a winter storm to bring his message of restoration to her.

Moments like that also linger with you and plant a desire to bring the life-changing message to more people.

CHAPTER 58

HIS NAME WAS ROY

WE WERE preparing a group of students with the School of Evangelism in New Hampshire. This school was a mission bridge school or a mini–Discipleship Training School for church folks who wanted to be equipped to share their faith. We had a wonderful team that would travel with us for the twelve weeks, leading small groups and helping to support and encourage the students.

On the first night of classes, Mike joined Linelle's small group, bringing a challenging dynamic from the start. He always seemed out of place and off-topic. He shared some of his life's challenges, emotional wounds from his tour in Vietnam, problems in life, and ongoing therapy for severe bouts of depression. He could never forgive himself for what he had done in war, for taking innocent lives in his rage. He was down on himself and on his life. Linelle shared her concerns with us; he wasn't connecting in class and seemed to miss the point each week.

Then came the outreach to New York. We were sure that would be too much for Mike and were shocked to see his name on the signup sheet. When he was going to go, we had a long pause about how we could support him and not have trouble on the trip because of his special issues and tendency to get sidetracked. It was a large group, and we had broken the students into eight teams. We placed Mike on the team with the easiest schedule and the most non-threatening situations and put some very committed leaders in charge.

The first outreach was such an exciting time for the students, and everyone found their way to the vans. They had all of their outreach supplies, and they were praying as they left. Mike's group pulled out, and we breathed a sigh of relief, confident that he was in the best situation for the evening.

Doug's team was the last to leave and headed for a difficult outreach location. Doug always seemed to choose the most challenging outreach places, and that night he was working with Pastor Ron from Brooklyn. The vans were loaded, and out of the building came Mike.

"Where is my team?" he asked. He had gone to have a smoke at the wrong time and missed their departure.

Now his problem had become our challenge. We could not leave him alone in the building. We could not take him to his team. So, he hopped into Doug's van. Joanne and Jacob were in the van and had been on outreach to New York many times with us. There were other seasoned and experienced leaders too. Doug made sure that Mike was going to be taken care of.

As the team unloaded the vans, they heard a call from a cardboard box—a homeless person's living space. "Jacob, Jacob... is that you?"

It was a man named Roy. The year before, JoAnne and Jacob had met Roy in another borough. They sat with him at a feeding ministry and at once felt compassion for him. He was a veteran who was still haunted by nightmares from his time in the war. He lived on the street, and they had reached out to him to no avail.

Roy told them that he could never follow Jesus and that he had secrets too awful to tell and was too far gone to be forgiven. He was punishing himself by choosing to live homeless. Their hearts were moved by him and it surprised them to see him again in a different part of the city among the eleven million people. They were amazed that he remembered them, even calling out Jacob's name.

"Roy, you remembered us. Wow, you don't know how many times we have prayed for you this year. We never thought we would see you again." Jake said in amazement and aware that the Lord was doing something special here. The circumstances of finding Roy again were just so random that God must have been working to bring him back to our team once again to hear of God's love.

"Roy, can't you see God sent us here again to tell you of his care for you?" Roy nodded in amazement. "What is keeping you from God's love?"

Then, with tears, Roy told his story. Many years ago, he was a young soldier in Vietnam. He saw a child running toward his men with a bomb strapped to his back. What an awful choice to take the life of an innocent child or take your life and the lives of others. His gun answered, and the child and bomb were gone. Yet the image of that, the injustice of it, the horror of war, had so devastated him he could not forgive himself. Every day he rehearsed that scene over and over in his mind, and it paralyzed him.

JoAnne and Jacob knelt on the sidewalk next to his makeshift box home and told him of God's unconditional love and forgiveness. Then they thought of Mike. He was unlikely to help, but they invited him into the conversation.

As Mike heard Roy's story, he related. He talked about forgiveness. As he did, a fresh understanding of his own life came to him. God's grace and forgiveness were enough, and the two men encountered God's love. Through their tears, they prayed to receive God's love and forgiveness. Through grace, they prayed to be forgiven, and they forgave themselves.

"When were you in Nam?" Mike asked. "Me too; that is when I was there."

"Where were you?"

"I was only a few miles from you. How strange that we met in the streets of New York twenty years later, broken men finding each other and God's forgiveness."

Pastor Ron saw the scene and overheard the conversation. "I was in Vietnam too. I was a helicopter pilot right in that same area and probably transported both of you."

Grace extended like this is beyond our understanding. God's love for a wounded soldier living on the streets of New York brings hope to another broken warrior. They found each other, and they found forgiveness. He shows them that nothing in their story was an accident, even Mike missing his assigned team. God wanted him, and even in his brokenness, He was going to use him to bring healing. That healing would wash over his sins too.

That moment brought healing to Mike's life in a way that years of self-hatred and counseling could not resolve. These three men hugging and rejoicing on the street corner were a testimony to God's amazing grace.

I have often thought of this amazing divine appointment, realizing that you don't have to be perfect to be God's ambassador; in fact, it is in our brokenness that God meets us, and as His grace flows through us to others, that healing finds us too.

CHAPTER 59

CHINA BIBLES

"WHEN YOU get to the security entrance, be careful not to say anything to alert the guards."

We didn't know what the situation would be. The Tiananmen Square protests had set off a cascade of other riots. The Chinese government's response was swift and devastating. Protestors were marked and arrested. Many disappeared without warning or a trace.

Our team had been preparing for this trip for months, but the situation in China had taken a more dangerous turn. From Hong Kong, we would send small teams, loaded down with Bibles, to several entry points. The underground Church in China was experiencing unprecedented growth. House churches with young leaders were popping up throughout the nation. The pastors were living in a dangerous environment. They needed Bibles to disciple the new believers, but the communist leaders considered Bibles to be pornography.

Special instructions were given to us during the training a few days earlier. If we made it through with our stash of Bibles, the next step would be to travel separately to different lockers where we would deliver our packages. The drop-off places were known to special couriers who would risk everything, including their lives, to pick up the Bibles and study books and distribute them to the waiting churches.

It was a dangerous operation—dangerous to western tourists and extremely dangerous to Chinese nationals who would retrieve them from the drop boxes. Now, with protests throughout the land, we weren't sure what scrutiny we would face at the border.

Judy, one of our team members, was carrying a package of Bibles, and she had her skirt filled with the Gospel of John tucked into the slot pockets sewn into her skirt. She was literally clothed in the Word of God. The guard immediately stopped Judy and demanded that she turn over her parcel. She began crying so loudly that he was embarrassed to have caused her to be so upset. She "lost face." To quiet her down, he gave the Bibles back and hurried her through the line.

Another member of the team had a boom box that was hollowed out and stuffed with the Bible portions. Doug's suit jacket also had special compartments filled with the scriptures.

The scene was especially tense that morning. The heat was sweltering, and Doug's full suit packed with Bibles was almost unbearable.

Sweat was trickling down his brow, and his collar was streaked.

"Next!" the guard growled, piercing eyes looking for any sign of a problem.

Soldiers carrying guns lined the catwalk overhead. It was so intimidating.

Doug handed his passport over. "Why are you coming to China?"

"Tourist." He had been instructed to say only what was necessary, not to offer any information or act nervous, and not to implicate anyone else on the team no matter what.

The guard stared at him and then demanded, "Give me your Bibles." They made him. Now he was not only sweating from the heat, but he was shaking from a combination of fear and the unknown.

Behind him on the street was an ice cream vendor. It was such an odd place for ice cream, but it was the perfect distraction. "Okay. Here are my Bibles. Can I buy you ice cream? And for all the guards, let me buy everyone some." All the guards came down and joined Doug for their dessert. During this distraction, the rest of the couriers passed through the line and into China.

Throughout the next week, this scene was repeated over and over at different checkpoints. The officers caught Doug almost every time, but the team brought in thousands of Bibles and study books.

CHAPTER 60

THAT DOESN'T WORK ANYMORE

WE WERE in Poland with a summer Joshua Generation youth outreach team. As we were setting up in a community to do a street drama and share the Gospel, several YWAMers came by. They were on outreach with the "Year with Jesus" program. They were at the end of their time in Poland.

Becky, one of the leaders, asked me, "What are you going to do here?"

I told her we would do a street mime that presented the Gospel, and then we would give an invitation and pray with those who responded to give their lives to Jesus.

She looked puzzled. "Well, I don't think that will work here. You have to build trusting relationships with people and have time to share your lives, and when you have earned the right to share, you can tell them about the Lord. We don't believe in this kind of street ministry."

I was surprised at her comment because we had spent the previous two weeks doing the same ministry throughout other cities and had prayed with hundreds of people from Poland and other European nations to receive Jesus.

I invited her to join us and to watch and help us. She seemed hesitant and maybe somewhat afraid to be associated with our team, not wanting us to do harm to anyone they had been sharing with, but she joined us. At the end of the drama, when the invitation was given, many people bowed their heads and prayed aloud as the translator led them in a prayer of salvation and commitment to Jesus as Lord.

As was our custom, after the group prayer, our team went among those who had prayed. We formed small teams, going over the Gospel using the wordless book. Becky joined one of the small groups and again prayed with those who responded. The people were very sincere, and many of them had tears in their eyes as they prayed aloud to receive Jesus.

Becky came up to me afterward and said how surprised she was that people had responded. I told her that the same scenario had happened over and over for the past three weeks in Poland. I had the same experience all over the world.

Becky had tears in her eyes. "Deb, I have been here for almost nine months on outreach, and my heart has been to see people come to know the Lord. I have befriended many people and have waited for the right moment to tell them about the Lord. Yet, I see that in just a few hours, these people have opened their hearts to Jesus. I feel like I might have missed so many opportunities, and now my time is almost over."

We prayed God would open opportunities for Becky to share with her Polish friends and make the most of the opportunities left for her.

Several days later, I got an email from Becky.

Do you remember me? The YWAMer from Nowy Sącz? After our talk, I went home and met with Mary, whom I had befriended that past year. I asked her if she wanted to hear the Gospel. She said yes. She joyfully responded prayed to receive Jesus.

I learned something today. Relationships are important, but God can make a way for us to tell people of His love in His timing, and we should always look for an opportunity to share. I pray that the Lord will use me in my last thirteen days here. I had always wanted to run away from street evangelism before, but when I saw your team and how they gave themselves to it, it made me understand how effective it could be.

Thank you for showing me that people will respond to the Gospel if we will just ask. It takes perseverance in some circumstances to find open hearts and to tell the message to be understood and received. Just as in fishing, there is a skill that is gained by watching how people respond, what questions are on their hearts, where they are hurting, and what holds them back from trusting the Lord.

There is so much spiritual static and confusion that it takes wisdom to speak to people's hearts so they can understand. Jesus may be the answer to our deepest needs, but each person is in a different place and has unique questions and needs. If you try to answer questions they might not be asking, your words will bounce off them.

The Holy Spirit is our teacher, and He will help us listen for the open door in people's lives.

PART SIX

1997 New Direction
YWAM Pittsburgh, Boston, Philadelphia

CHAPTER 61

I WANT TO BE YOUR INTIMATE FRIEND

IF YOU read a textbook about children of alcoholics, I have most of the typical traits of a child raised by an alcoholic father. I was reserved. My chosen way to process pain was to live with numbness.

One exception to this was with my family. From day one, I was bonded to my children with a deep love. Our marriage was close and a safe place of peace and love for me.

"I am just not a very emotional person," I often told my friends, who commented on my detachment in many situations that should have merited tears. I acted with compassion; I just felt only a little compassion.

When I turned forty, I had an encounter with the Lord. I was teaching first grade, and a group of mothers of my students invited me to a Christmas party. They surprised me with a cake and presents. Snow fell during our get-together, and the ride home was a typical New England drive on icy roads. The driver stopped at the bottom of our driveway, unwilling to drive into my steep, snow-covered lane.

Anita, one of the mothers, was sitting with me in the back of the car. She stopped me before I exited the car and said she wanted to pray for me. I was uncomfortable, but I agreed. "God has a word for you. He wants to be your intimate friend."

I didn't know what that meant. Why would God say that to me, anyway? Wasn't I living a committed life already?

My walk up the hill to our house was slow, with me stopping every few feet to take in the surrounding beauty. A full moon illuminated the path. Trees were bending, sometimes cracking, under the weight of the falling snow. In that solitude, the words continued to come back to my mind again and again—I want to be your intimate friend.

Later that night, it was so quiet, and the words were so loud, still resonating through my heart. A warm, almost electric feeling flooded through me. I had never felt that before, and I wasn't sure what was happening to me. I woke Doug up and tried to explain what had happened to me. He summed it up like this: "These things always happen to me in God's presence. That is a normal thing."

It wasn't normal for me at all. For three months, whenever I would think about that moment or even the words "intimate friend," the presence of God would flood over me and through me every day, throughout the day, and always with the same message to my mind and spirit. I was being pursued, and I was awakening to a new place in my walk with the Lord.

Then one day, it didn't happen anymore. But the memory stayed with me. I never knew why that happened or why it ended, but I knew it was real.

Several years later, I knelt in my bedroom, peering through my French doors into the beautiful autumn scene outside, and I whispered an honest prayer: "I am in some way disconnected, Lord. I will serve You all the days of my life, and I will obey You. I find joy in my life in many ways, yet there is still a place of disconnect. I accept that the wounds of my childhood may have changed the wiring of my emotions.

"When everyone around me is worshiping, I sing, but I never feel anything. I still sing, though, because You are worthy. Worship is about who He is, not how we feel. When people need comfort, I hold them in my arms and pray my best prayer for Your tender care, but I am often detached from them. I don't expect that I will ever change. Maybe I don't have faith, or maybe it is just your plan, but if it is possible, could you please rewire my heart? I will walk any path, confident that You know who I am and will be with me."

A few months later, I was speaking to our church, a megachurch that seldom gave women the microphone. I grabbed that opportunity to talk about having an authentic relationship with God.

"Jesus will be near you, intimately acquainted with your deepest needs and desires. He will be with you in the joys and sorrows of life. You can reach out to Him in the heartbreak, joy, and each moment." And somewhere in the message, I shared, "He will be with you at the graveside." I did not understand what I was saying, but shortly after, it became prophetic, I remembered my prayer—if it is possible, could you please rewire my heart. Even at the graveside?

God answered my prayer in 1997 in a way I would never have chosen. My father died on September 16, 1996. Our daughters both got engaged at Thanksgiving. My mother fell ill in January. She died on April 11, 1997. I took care of her during the last weeks of her life, alone except for the visiting hospice nurses who bathed her and gave her increasing doses of morphine. Our daughters got married in a double wedding on May 16, 1997, and moved in different directions, far from me. We left our friends, our home, and the ministry that had been our foundation for eighteen years. We moved to Pittsburgh from Manchester, New Hampshire, into a friend's home that was empty and waiting to be sold. I lost both of my parents, my home, my friends, our ministry and my family unit. It was an emotional tsunami.

At that moment, sitting with my mother, as frail, quiet, and needy as she was, I knew I had a choice. I could handle it with a disconnected heart, but it would be painful. I could do what I knew I should: feed her, comb her hair, cover her while she slept, or I could take a risk and engage. I made a choice that day that allowed God to heal my broken heart. I sat in bed with her, held her close through the hours, talked to her, prayed over her, and let myself feel the grief. It was devastating. Later, I understood it was my healing. I had experienced some sort of heart transplant.

After all the losses that year, I was in Pittsburgh with a new teaching job. During the teacher's prep time, I tried to set up my classroom, but I couldn't find the energy to put decorations on the bulletin boards. I just sat there. I played worship music to fill the time, and I realized that if I couldn't staple construction paper on the wall, how would I find the strength to live my life?

My friend, John, struggled with an extreme immune deficiency for his whole life. A doctor in Boston suggested he consider a bone marrow transplant to restore his immune system. He took a step of faith, and the process was so difficult. His old system had to be completely destroyed for new life and blood cells to take its place. The process was hard to watch and very hard for him to walk through, but in the end, his body had to be renewed.

Emotional healing can sometimes be like that. For me, God brought me through an intense series of crises and led me to a place where He could restore my emotional makeup.

In the end, I too was restored to a place of wholeness. Each day I was in a new place, my care for people was sincere and from a healed heart. My love for God was more than obedience and commitment, it was with a heart that responded to His love for me. The Lord did what seemed impossible in response to my honest prayer.

CHAPTER 62

1997

ON OUR way to Target World in Atlanta with the Joshua Generation teens, we stopped in Pittsburgh. I was thankful to have a brief visit with my parents. Our house in Webster wasn't fancy, but it was home to me. As I arrived in front of the house, I could see my dad sitting on the front porch, slightly slumped over. I called him, but he didn't respond. I guessed he was sleeping.

My parents loved gardening, but their usual vegetable garden was missing. That was the first time in my life I had seen that happen. Over the years, his garden was a source of enjoyment for him, and he cared for it diligently. His tomatoes grew from special seeds given to him by an elderly Italian friend. He saved the seeds each year for the next planting. We often received boxes of tomatoes in the mail from him. Those packages were a way of expressing love to us. He once grew a three-pound tomato that was featured in a gardening magazine.

That year, Dad had been too weak to plant, and the empty garden space was one of the glaring signs that his life was slipping away. As I walked along the pathway alongside the house, a familiar aroma filled the air: gardenias. Their porch was decked with two very large gardenia plants. Those beautiful flowering plants were difficult to grow. It was a signature of my mother's love for beautiful things.

She met me at the door and, after a greeting, warned me about my father's condition as he sat on the porch. "Don't be alarmed. It is just a progression of the disease. He is not in any pain." Her warning could not have prepared me for the impact of seeing him there.

He looked up and nodded, acknowledging me, but didn't say a word. The electro-larynx tool he used to talk lay on the table beside him. It made him sound like a robot since his voice box was removed. It was too much of an effort to raise it to his throat to speak. There was a worn crossword puzzle book next to it and a Number 2 yellow pencil that was worn almost flat from use. He spent his days doing mindless puzzles, his mind slipping away with the hours.

I filled the space with a conversation about our family, how the children were doing in school, and my plans for the summer.

"Your gardenias smell like heaven."

His half-opened eyes now brightened up a little. They say the eyes are a window to the soul. His eyes were hollow now.

I knew that would be the last time I saw my father. I wanted to remember that last embrace. My mother walked me to the car and waved until I was out of sight.

In September, she called me with concern. Our home was full of hunting and fishing equipment. There was a special chest of drawers built by my grandfather Daugherty for guns. The drawers were lined with a special felt. His vast gun collection was safely stored in them. When the social worker stopped by earlier, she warned my mother to remove the guns from the house, which she did.

The next day, my father went into a rage and was looking for his guns. The police came and took him away in a straitjacket to a nursing facility. Days later, my father found peace in the presence of the Lord. I thought about God's faithfulness to touch his life, the miracle of forgiveness, salvation, and a changed destiny.

CHAPTER 63

THANKSGIVING

THANKSGIVING that fall was a very special time for our daughters. Rachel met Aaron at Concord Christian School in high school. She was finishing her senior year at Bentley College. Aaron had asked Doug several times for his blessing for them to get engaged. Chuck met Bethany at Boston University, and he was now finishing his senior year before joining the Marine Corps. He also asked Doug to bless their engagement. The answer for both young men had been, "Not yet."

I was amazed at their patience. We loved both young men and were thankful our daughters had found them. At Thanksgiving, Doug felt peace about welcoming both guys to the family. My mom was on the phone listening when they proposed officially in the dining room before we served the turkey.

It was a moment of joy for her after my father's death. She looked forward to the wedding. We made the trip back to the Mon Valley for Christmas. Throughout all our years of traveling and moving, Christmas was a time for family, and we never missed spending it there.

CHAPTER 64

CHRISTMAS

MY MOM seemed very sentimental during the visit. Living alone was taking a toll on her in ways I couldn't describe, but I knew something beyond grief was happening to her.

Christmas Eve was always a time to open presents from the grandparents, but that year, Mom sat all her grandkids down.

"It's been a difficult few months, and I realize even more now how special you all are to me. I want you to have something from my home. You can choose anything, big or small. Something that reminds you of being with Grandpa and me, something of your childhood."

With that, our children went walking through the house. They were thoughtful and quiet. "I'll take this cedar chest! It reminds me of being here." Bethany spoke up. Rachel chose the wicker rocker that my mom had held her in many times. Jeremy chose a dog knickknack that was positioned on the bookshelf. Douglas took a metal dog-shaped nutcracker. I don't think anyone thought about value; they thought about memories.

After we returned home from this trip, I called Mom and noticed she seemed to have a severe cold. I was concerned that I might have given her a virus. A few days later, I called, and she sounded weaker. In the middle of the call, there was a bang and the sound of something hitting the wall.

290 - A LEGACY OF FAITH

"Mom, are you alright?"

There was no response. I called my friend, Donna Britt, and she drove over to check on her. Donna found her passed out on the floor with the phone dangling and tapping into the wall. An ambulance came and took her to the hospital.

We drove back to Pennsylvania. Was it the flu? A stroke? The twelve-hour trip from New Hampshire left a lot of time for speculation. We rushed through the Mon Valley Hospital and found her room. She was asleep and looked so frail and worn out. The nurse told us to expect the doctor any minute.

When he walked into the room, the doctor was reading the lab reports on her chart. Then he looked up and cried, "Oh no. Estelle. How can this be?" He immediately recognized her. My mom called him by name; he was the oncologist who cared for my father just months before.

"What's wrong, doctor? Do I have a severe case of the flu?"

He gulped and took a deep breath. "No, dear lady. This is not the flu. You have stage-four lung cancer, and it is in your ribs. I am so sorry." He tried to fight back the tears, but they were overflowing down his cheeks.

It was a diagnosis that none of us expected. They later informed us that there wasn't any treatment possible and that the disease was so advanced that Mom only had a few months to live. I stayed with her during the day, and my brothers helped trade off in the evenings. She was wrestling with the news and the choices that she had to make.

"I want to be at home," she pleaded.

So, we brought her home for her last goodbyes.

I spent the next few weeks with my mother. Those intimate moments of caring for her took me to a place of the deepest grief, but also a place of restoration. Those days were a gift from heaven for us both.

> *My frame was not hidden from You when I was made in the secret place, when I was woven together in the depths of the earth. Your eyes saw my unformed body; all the days ordained for me were written in Your book before one of them came to be. How precious to me are Your thoughts, God! How vast is the sum of them!*
> Psalm 139:15–17 NIV

At her funeral, there were many people whom I had never met.

"How did you know my mom?" I asked them.

"She was my friend and would help me pick out presents at the gift shop at Central Pharmacy."

"Your mom prayed for me in the card aisle when my husband was sick."

"When I heard your mother's testimony, I decided to become a Christian. I was filled with the Holy Spirit when she prayed with me in the back room of the gift shop."

CHAPTER 65

YWAM PITTSBURGH

I'VE BEEN told never to make a significant life decision during a life crisis. Still, sometimes the turmoil forces you to choose. After our daughters' double wedding, we met with Pastor Ken Anderson. All the changes caused us to reflect on what we wanted to do in the next chapter of our lives. Grandma Daugherty, my mom's mother, was ninety-four years old. We had lived away from the Mon Valley for eighteen years, and we felt it was time to come home for a season.

There wasn't a plan or a timetable; we just knew it was a new chapter for us. In the previous 16 years, we had the privilege to train and mobilize many Christians to share their faith. The Body of Christ had worked together with the Crisis Pregnancy Centers, the March for Life, and the March for Jesus. The Power Team Crusade had brought the state together for an event, and we had a deep peace that our time in New Hampshire was ending.

"Pastor Ken, it has been a privilege to serve with you for these years," Doug said. "After losing Deb's parents and the many changes happening in our family with our daughters getting married and many projects being finished, we are praying about moving back to the Pittsburgh area to be closer to our families. We don't have a timetable in mind."

Pastor Ken seemed surprised, and his response was very abrupt. "Okay, we do our annual budget in July, and you will have your last check at the end of the month." That sealed our timetable; we would leave in July. During the last weeks of her life, it was one of the few times in my life that I needed a pastor. Those lonely weeks sitting by myself, missing my family, and struggling with the grief were beyond what I could handle. Doug was holding our family in New Hampshire together, keeping the boys in school, and helping with the wedding plans for the girls. He tried hard to be supportive, but he needed support too.

My friend, Tom Murphy, an elder from our church, called during those last days with my mom. He cared for us and expressed his concern. "Has the pastor called you?"

"Not yet," I replied.

Five minutes later, the phone rang again. "Hello, Deb, it is Pastor Ken. I wanted to call and pray for you."

I was grateful for the call even though I knew Tom had prompted him to reach out.

It was business as usual when I returned to my job in the church office after my mom's funeral. I had given twelve years of my life to serve in the church as a teacher in the Christian school, a leader in the inner circle of the decision-making committees, and a pastor's wife. After all that investment, I wondered how I wasn't on the pastor's radar when I needed it most. I don't know what I expected that first morning back, but my world had been turned upside down, and my heart was broken. It seemed no one was even aware of it.

I gave my most creative energy and time because I believed in what we were doing as a church. I realized that serving in a megachurch is more like being involved with a business. Your contribution is valued, but you are more of a partner than part of a family. I accepted it, not with anger but more with sadness.

I had been a part of many smaller fellowship groups over the years that were family: California Fellowship, Power Group and Lighthouse. Those groups were knit together and bonded with love and commitment. My assumption that FCC was the same was wrong.

It was just too large to have those kinds of intimate friendships.

That helped me understand Pastor Ken's reaction and how matter-of-fact he was to send us on our way. It also helped me see God was leading us on, even though I was still very fragile.

Doug and I sat down and dreamed about what the future might hold. "What has God prepared us to do? What is in our hearts?"

The first thing I was sure about was that I would not be working in a megachurch ministry. I needed community. I was also sure that the ministry I most felt at home with was YWAM, even though our departure in 1981 had been hard. We had maintained relationships with the leaders, and there were genuine friendships there.

We called Dave Adams, the Northeast YWAM director, and asked for a meeting. On the ferry from Connecticut to New York, we planned what had been brewing in our hearts. "Dave, we would like to pioneer a YWAM base in the Pittsburgh area." The irony wasn't lost on Dave. Eighteen years earlier, he had been on the leadership team that asked us to leave the mission. Now, he was the leader who welcomed us back. It was family.

Our next call was to Pastor John and Sandy Derrico, who had been the ministers at the Christian Center since 1998. Doug was ordained in a service with him before we left for Europe in 1979. They were friends for life! They had a shared history and a deep trust in each other. Pastor John welcomed us and offered that the church had room to start YWAM on the property. Barry and Terri Zungre heard we were coming and offered for us to land in their house until we could find a place to live. Their friendship and support were essential to this next chapter. We had a location, and we had relationships. That is part of the foundation for pioneering a new ministry.

CHAPTER 66

ISRAEL

FOR MANY Christians, a trip to this historical nation is on their bucket list. It allows them to walk where Jesus walked and see the places mentioned in the Bible. Our Discipleship Training School's 2002 outreach to Israel was a trip of a lifetime for us all.

Doug had the privilege of having both of our sons, Douglas and Jeremy, with him on this trip. This is his story, and it is amazing.

During the months of preparation, our staff and students heard from several "experts" about doing outreach in Israel. They memorized passages from the Old Testament. We hoped to convince the Jewish people Jesus was the Messiah. Our team was ready to engage in conversation, confident that they could share the Gospel. Our expert trainers cautioned us to have low expectations, though, because people were not open to the Gospel.

Right away, the team realized that approach wasn't working. While most Jewish people had a strong cultural identity with Israel, their knowledge of the Hebrew Scriptures was minimal. In fact, they could be identified as non-spiritual. Many claimed to be atheists. After several days of struggling, the team had to reevaluate how to witness in Israel. The conversations resembled those of Paul on Mars Hill rather than Peter preaching to the religious people of his time.

Few people listened to them in those first few days, so each evening the team would debrief. They discussed what approach would be helpful to even talk to people about spiritual things. Apologetics seemed to be one key to laying a foundation for faith.

They were told that any street meeting would cause a strong pushback, even a dangerous response. "You can't do that here."

When our team prayed, the word the Lord was: "You MUST do this here, openly and courageously."

The "Doors" drama helped to start conversations. Apologetics laid the groundwork for conversations about faith. Personal testimonies opened the door for the presentation of the Gospel.

"Jesus was a historical person. He walked on these streets. He claimed to be the Messiah and God. I have experienced a personal relationship with him, and he has changed my life."

Soon, the Holy Spirit was working to open hearts to hear the Good News. Each day, people prayed to accept and trust Jesus as their Lord and Savior. On the streets of all the major cities, the team performed and shared the Gospel.

We heard of a pastor from Donora, a small town in the Mon Valley, who had a Filipino church in a red-light district in Tel Aviv. That location was the site of many bombings and terrorist attacks. He invited our team, and Doug felt in his heart that we should go.

"I know this is one of the most dangerous places. I am going tonight, but I want to give you all the freedom to stay back. You won't be thought of as less if you decide to stay."

Everyone stepped up, despite tangible fears, and affirmed, "We will go with you."

The scene outside was worse than any news report. Terrorists had had blown up many of the buildings. Debris filled the streets. The people on the streets spoke eight languages. We had translators, and we divided the crowd into groups to hear the Gospel. After the drama

"Doors," we prayed with many people. The pastor had an underground church; it was literally underground.

Amanda, one student, proclaimed, "We faced fear in the face, and fear ran away!" She told us she was deeply affected by the courage of the other YWAMers, the pastor, and the open hearts of the people we met there.

A few days before Christmas, we heard a rumor that CNN was going to set up cameras in Bethlehem on Christmas Eve. They had only allowed Arabs into the city at the time, so Doug and the team entered through the open door into our Lord's birthplace.

A school bus picked them up. It was full of other believers, and on the way through the streets, Doug looked up and saw that there were anti-aircraft guns on the rooftops. Enormous pictures of Yasser Arafat draped the buildings. Conversations on the bus were about what they hoped to do once in the city: prayer walks and photo opportunities.

Doug spoke up, "We are going to present the Gospel and preach right there in the streets." Our team heard a collective gasp all around the bus.

"Sir, you are out of your mind. You cannot do that. You will start a riot and maybe get shot." Their objections only reinforced Doug's resolve.

"Are you intending to preach on the street?" One passenger asked. "These people all speak Arabic."

Doug answered, "Yes, we are going to do this, but we don't have an Arabic translator."

The man replied, "I speak Arabic. I will translate for you. If you are crazy enough to do this, I will stand beside you."

As the crowd gathered around when the drama began, they were pushing so close that the team hardly had room to move. The Palestine Liberation Organization (PLO) was policing the area and came to see what the commotion was about. They took positions to give us room and pushed back the crowd of Palestinian men.

"Jesus said I am the way, the truth and the life," Doug shouted over the sound system.

The crowd grew quiet and listened to hear more. Our new Arabic translator shouted louder than Doug.

"قال يسوع أنا الطريق الحق الحياة و."

"No man comes to the Father but through Jesus." Doug continued to give a Gospel message and invitation. "If you want to receive Jesus as your only Savior, raise your hand." Throughout the crowd, men were lifting their hands. It seemed the courage they saw in each other emboldened them. The PLO soldiers quickly moved through the crowd and were pushing their hands down.

The team had boxes of Arabic Bibles on the bus, and Doug approached the PLO captain and asked, "We have free books to give away. Can you assist us?" He agreed, not realizing they were the Scriptures, and 600 men received Bibles.

Our Savior came to that village as a newborn baby, and 2000 years later, He came to the hearts of men who heard about Him for the first time.

CHAPTER 67

NEW YORK OUTREACH

"ARE YOU feeling okay?" I asked Doug. He seemed extra exhausted and foggy in his mind. On the ride home from doing some last-minute shopping for our mission trip to New York, his driving seemed off. He was slower than normal; he made a left-hand turn from the right lane and even sat at a light that had turned green for almost a minute.

Was it relapsing malaria again? He had suffered from many recurrences of the disease for nine years. It started during his first mission trip to Liberia.

Several doctors could not diagnose it. The parasite was only visible in a blood test at the height of the infection. All the lab results came back inconclusive. I recognized the symptoms—exhaustion, struggling to decide, fever, aches, and trouble breathing.

Overnight, the same familiar fever and shaking chills began. We were to leave in the morning with a team from Walnut Grove AG church. It was an outreach after an eight-week School of Evangelism. I questioned whether he could make it with the team, but he shut down any consideration of staying back. Thankfully, it seemed like one of the milder recurrences.

On the drive to the city, he slept most of the time. I explained before we left, he wasn't feeling well and that we recognized what was happening, so the team wouldn't be overly focused on him. He was determined to still take part as much as he was able.

The weekend was packed full of people sharing the Gospel. We worked with established New York ministries, and our team had many opportunities to put into practice the things they learned in the evangelism training class. Many people responded by receiving Jesus. Doug put in his best effort and tried to take part, but he was suffering the whole time.

"How long has Doug been having these attacks?" Mary asked on the ride home. I gave her a brief explanation of what had happened.

"I am surprised that this was never diagnosed and treated. Both my husband and I were missionaries and have had malaria. The symptoms you describe are consistent with this illness. I am sure my husband could help."

She gave me the information for Dr. Markle's office, and Doug went to see him several days later. He explained to Doug how difficult it was to catch the malaria parasite in a blood test and that it was understandable that he had not been diagnosed until then. We were relieved to have a doctor who was experienced in recognizing and treating the infection. When the prescribed medication was finished, we were relieved that Doug would not have to suffer from it again.

CHAPTER 68

2003 LIBERIA

WHEN OUR Discipleship Training School with YWAM Pittsburgh was praying about where to go for their outreach, Liberia came up in the times of intercession. We contacted our friend, Pastor Sydney Thomas, and he agreed to help us with the plans. The staff and students were excited about the opportunity. Our son, Douglas, and his friend, Mark Cornacchione, were students in the DTS.

From the moment I heard about it, I had concerns. Doug's previous trips happened during the civil war, and the country was still unstable, with Charles Taylor still trying to take over the country.

The plan was to use the drama "Doors" in the streets during the day and show the Jesus Film in the fields in the evenings. An engineer developed a fifteen-foot screen we could disassemble and carry in a hockey bag. A generator and video camera setup would let us project onto the screen, which people could view from both sides, doubling the capacity for crowds.

Before the trip, the staff and students struggled with the finances for the outreach. We prayed each day for the funds to come in, but one week out, we still needed $22,000. It was a sobering moment. We would have to cancel the trip. As I was working in the accounting office, one of our students came in and confided that he had the funds to cover the shortfall. His generous heart and willingness to give amazed me. But I hesitated to let him make the gift. God always has what we need to do His work. The struggle of having faith in finances is part of learning to trust His character and being willing to do what we can in each circumstance. I told him to wait and see. I thanked him for his willingness. The funds came in through different sources, and they were all provided before the team left. All $22,000!

The outreach was the most fruitful we had ever experienced. During the day, crowds would watch the drama "Doors" and respond to the message. In the evenings, the team would set up the screen in the middle of a field. Shortly after, thousands would gather to watch the story of Jesus. At the crucifixion scene, the team would pause the film, and Doug would give an invitation. Thousands responded at every show. Twenty-two thousand people gave their hearts to Jesus during that amazing outreach. It was the exact finances we trusted God for in the last weeks.

Back in Pittsburgh, we continued to get reports of the amazing move of the Holy Spirit to bring people to salvation. I continued to be concerned for the safety of my husband and son. Doug returned a week ahead of the team. When I picked him up at the airport, I found out that my greatest fears had become a reality. He stepped out of the customs room and was so frail-looking, barely able to walk.

"I want to see my parents," he requested. I was hesitant, but he insisted on going from the airport to his parent's home. When we walked in, he hugged his mom and dad, almost fainting, and mumbled, "Take me to Dr. Markle's office."

"How long have you been ill?" I asked. I was very concerned. I had seen him with malaria many times, but that seemed worse than the worst time. He had been sick for more than a week but pushed through because of the ministry work that had been happening.

When we walked into Dr. Markle's, he immediately called for an ambulance, and the nurse started an IV. For the next three days, Doug

DEBRA TUNNEY - 305

lay almost lifeless in his hospital bed, his fever spiking throughout the day. The medication seemed to not be helping. All the many articles I had read about malaria being a killer played like a tape in my mind. I was worried about the trip from the beginning. He had just been treated for his nine-year-recurring infection, but this was a new one, possibly a different strain.

"Dr. Markle, he is going to be okay, right? The medication you are giving him can cure this. Isn't that true? I shouldn't be worried, right?" My words were filled with anxiety, and I was waiting for an assurance that I hoped he could give me.

"We have found the parasite in the bloodwork and can confirm it as malaria," he calmly replied. "We are treating him with every drug available. He's getting excellent care. So, we are doing everything medically for him. When I go home at night, my wife, Mary, and I spend time on our knees, asking God to bring healing to him. Our trust is in the Lord." Dr. Markle's calm countenance and words of hope helped me to take a breath.

My trust was in the Lord as well, but I also knew that things do not always work out as you pray and hope for. The next morning, Doug responded and could carry on a conversation with me. We learned that the preventive medication the team had taken was for those who live in the country and have long-term exposure. The drug was not for short-term mission trips, and our team was not adequately protected.

The phone in Doug's hospital room rang. It was an emergency phone call from Pastor Sydney Thomas in Liberia. "We are sorry to tell you that your son, Douglas, is gravely ill with malaria. He is in the best clinic, and we are giving him the best possible medical treatment available here in Liberia. He has not been responding, so we are very concerned."

My husband was recovering, and our son could die in another country. My heart was beating so fast that I could almost hear it. We prayed in the McKeesport hospital, and at the same time, Mark and the team were praying with our son. When Mark saw Douglas, he was shocked at his condition. His fever was spiking, and his body was discolored, turning a sort of yellow that comes when organs shut down. The team's immediate response was to call out to the Lord for mercy.

"Lord, please save his life," we prayed. Sometimes desperate prayers are all you can offer. The IV pole holding the fluids for Douglas was labeled "Donated from the Hitchcock Clinic, New Hampshire." It was part of the medical supplies that Hitchcock Clinic had contributed many years before and was sent in a container by our church, the Faith Christian Center.

Immediately, Douglas felt strength returning to his body. God's healing touch was restoring him. Within a few hours, he was on his way to recovery. Thankfully, he did not have any relapses. The Christian faith doesn't mean you are insulated from trouble. God cares, and we can be sure He hears our prayers and will respond with great compassion to our needs.

CHAPTER 69

BOSTON

RAMONA MUSCH, the YWAM Northeast Director, was faithful in bringing the leaders together for times of encouragement and vision for our district. We had the gathering in 2005 in New York. It had been inspiring to gather with the other base leaders. In our prayer times, we prayed about new bases. We mentioned Boston. In fact, we always mentioned Boston at the meetings. There had been four, maybe five, previous attempts to start YWAM there. The pioneering teams had prayed and worked to build a network and asked God for His plans for reaching the city.

On our drive home, we talked about it. YWAM Pittsburgh was established. We felt confident that the team there would continue to train new missionaries to reach the community and send teams around the world. "I wonder who God will send to Boston. I think it is time for this to happen."

The pioneers would have to be ready to take on such a challenging location. They would need to be experienced and tenacious. New England was a challenging place to start new ministries. We heard of many who came to Boston with deep pockets and big visions, only to pack up a year later because it was too hard.

Pioneering in Boston would be challenging. It takes a special combination: a network of friends, financial supporters, and prayer supporters. We knew about that from living in New Hampshire for eighteen years. The leader would have to understand the city and have a heart for the needs of the people. Doug had worked in Boston for many years in our cleaning business and had prayed through the streets, asking God to move in the city. As we continued to identify who might be called, equipped and prepared to do it, we looked at each other.

"I think it is us!"

That was it. We knew we had a new assignment. During the next few months, we made several trips to Boston. We prayed in the Common, a public park, with the other New England leaders, who were now fully supporting us in our new adventure.

During these prayer times, I found this verse that describes David. Then one of the servants answered and said,

> "Look, I have seen a son of Jesse the Bethlehemite, who is skillful in playing, a mighty man of valor, a man of war, prudent in speech, and a handsome person; and the LORD is with him."
> 1 Samuel 16:18

The verse came alive to me. The Lord was giving us our focus. He would bring young people like David: artists, musicians, warriors, communicators, and charismatic people. And the Lord would be with them.

We prayed about whom to invite to our pioneering team.

Right away, I thought of Jessi Welsh (now Cieply). She was one of our closest friends and was a part of the leadership of YWAM in Pittsburgh. Several summers before, she had been with me on a trip to Boston to look for host churches for Joshua Generation. We sat in a coffee shop in the Boston Common after sharing at The Tremont Temple. She stared out the window at the busy street and park.

"You know, I have this feeling about this place. I can see myself living here." I wondered if God was speaking to her about the city, but now I believed she would be a part of the team. She was a 1 Samuel 16:18 follower of Jesus.

"Absolutely, I will," was her enthusiastic response.

Jeremy, our son, and Kandia were recently married. Their initial response was reserved, but they agreed to pray. When Gwen Bergquist asked Jeremy years ago about his future, his reply was, "I love evangelism, missions, traveling, and new things." God had prepared him. Kandia was an artist and a dancer who had a degree in ministry. She was passionate about seeing the arts in ministry. When they responded yes, I knew our team would be strong.

Jessica Kopacz was a New Englander with excellent organizational skills. She had worked with Child Evangelism Fellowship. She was ready for a new adventure and wanted to be closer to her family.

On October 6, 2006, our overfull moving van pulled out of our driveway on Finley Road in Belle Vernon and headed for Boston.

CHAPTER 70

THE CHAIR

FIVE TEAMS had attempted to put down roots for YWAM in Boston. Mark and Donna Britt, our friends, had spent several years building relationships and laying a prayer foundation for a missionary training base many years before. We were grateful for the goodwill and connections from their time in Boston. They prepared the way for us. Yet we knew it would be more challenging for us.

When friends and strangers heard of our plan to move to Boston, they would often remark with a guarded concern at how difficult it was to begin new ministries there.

"Oh, the people are so difficult there."

"The frozen chosen church doesn't make room for newcomers."

"Do you know the reputation New England has for being a killer of ministries?"

"It is so expensive to live. Don't be surprised if you can't pull this off!"

We heard different versions of these remarks from so many people. They reminded me of the report in Numbers 13 when the ten spies came back from a forty-day scouting trip to the Promised Land. Even though the land was flowing with milk and honey, they were gripped with fear facing the giants.

312 - A LEGACY OF FAITH

> *"We cannot go, they are stronger than us. We were like*
> *grasshoppers in our own sight."*
> Numbers 13:33

Fear distorts reality. Yes, there would be challenges ahead, but the grasshopper perspective was far from reality.

Those spies had seen the miraculous deliverance from Egypt through the Red Sea. God had promised an inheritance for them in the Promised Land. Yet, those reports reflected that their focus was on their strength and not on the Lord.

Caleb and Joshua saw the challenge through a different lens. Yes, there were giants. "We must take possession of the land. We can conquer it!" Caleb proclaimed in the face of adversity. He was confident in the Lord who had called them and who had promised to be with them.

God honored their faith, and forty years later, He led them to their inheritance. We focused on God's calling and trusted in His ability to make a way for us even with the challenges ahead.

Our first challenge was to find housing for our team. That was a significant giant. Housing costs in Boston were ten times higher than in the Mon Valley. Reading through the rental listing brought a bit of a sticker shock to us. We needed the first and last month's rent and a security deposit at the signing of a lease.

Our friends, Harry and Barbara Shepler, welcomed us to stay in their home about an hour from Boston. The rest of the team found a large apartment outside of the city as well. That gave us some breathing room and time to find a more reasonable place and save the funds needed to move to the city. We prayed, planned, and took many trips into the city.

Barry and Terri Zungre were lifelong friends who were in our Power Group thirty years earlier. Barry was a business owner in

Pittsburgh. They had been YWAM missionaries in Holland. Their commitment to stand with us encouraged us.

"I am with you all the way on this adventure. I know you are going to make it, regardless. You are determined, and I know God has called you." Those words of affirmation came back to us many times.

"You are to first serve and not look to lead" was the word Doug got in one of our prayer times. So, we looked for ways to serve. Linda Clark, one of the recognized prayer warriors of the city, invited us to her home. She was packing to move, but she made time to receive us and encourage us. "Thank you for coming to my city. We need you here. You are welcome here!" She prayed over us and offered her friendship.

As we said our parting goodbye, Doug inquired, "Is there anything we can do to help you?"

"Yes, as you can see, I am moving. My family has lived here for decades, and our attic is full. Most of it needs to be discarded. It would be so wonderful if you could help me," she replied.

Our team spent the next week in her attic. Linda encouraged us to take anything of value that we might need. When the last box was moved to the street for pickup, we knew our time had been a spiritual service. We had a new friend, and serving was our calling. We kept three brown wicker boxes, which for us would be a memory of that time.

After several months, we took a step and moved into a large house. The double rent and security took every dollar we had as a team, and for many reasons, it wasn't a long-term place for YWAM to be planted. The heat on the first floor didn't work, and the landlord didn't respond to our many requests for it to be repaired. We felt like the frozen chosen!

Doug was always on the lookout for furniture or tools left on the curb. This was a college city, with people frequently moving. When

314 - A LEGACY OF FAITH

people move out of the city, they often leave useful items out for others to pick up on the curb. *Curb Side Christmas* was a hobby for him.

"Check out what I found today!" he exclaimed as he dragged the ugliest green rocking chair out of our van. "I can't wait to refinish this! See this scratch? It is white oak."

I rolled my eyes and gave a deep sigh. First, it was a not-needed item. Second, it was ugly, with many layers of paint. Refinishing chairs was nowhere on our top priority list. He had never refinished a chair in his life.

"This is going to be beautiful. Just wait!" That was his last comment before taking off to Home Depot to get the tools and chemicals to restore the chair.

While he was loading up his cart with chair refinishing items, an elderly man stopped him and asked if he knew how to refinish floors.

"Yes, I have refinished many floors. Here are the things you need."

A minute later, he asked Doug the same question. This time, Doug filled his cart and wished him well.

"What do you mean?" the man stammered. "Can you explain that again? My name is Mike."

'You've come to serve!' came to Doug's mind.

"Okay, Mike. What floor do you need to refinish?" Mike explained he had a rental property, and he was trying to refinish the floors but didn't know how to do it. Doug followed him to the house and offered to do the job himself. No charge.

No charge sounded good to Mike, so Doug spent the next week stripping, sanding, and refinishing the floor. "All done, Mike. When will someone move into your place?"

"Oh, I don't have anyone yet. Are you looking for a place?" Mike also had two other apartments, and we rented all three. The price was one-third of what we were paying and three times the size. Our first discipleship training school happened in those apartments. "You came to serve" was the door to our first geographic footprint in Boston. The chair was refinished and was a special reminder to us of God's faithfulness when we work out His Word to us.

CHAPTER 71

THE UNION OYSTER HOUSE

"LOREN CUNNINGHAM is coming to Boston. Can you set up a few meetings for him?" His assistant asked, and, of course, we said yes. It would be an honor to have him in our city. When we asked if he could help us with a fundraiser, he said yes!

The Union Oyster House is the most historic restaurant in Boston, located on the Freedom Trail. We booked into the Heritage Room. Loren would give a brief message, and we would share the vision of YWAM Boston. Every one of the thirty-five seats was taken by new and old friends.

"You are going to need three containers," Loren instructed for the offering. "One for pledges, one for checks, and one for cash." We knew that our wicker boxes were the perfect containers to receive this first offering to launch the ministry.

"Just ask the Lord what He would have you give." Loren encouraged our guests. The next few minutes were quiet as, one by one, our guests brought their offerings to the three baskets. We counted ten thousand, twenty, sixty, all the way to ninety thousand! We were stunned at their generosity. There was an offering from Loren and the six members of our team. We were in this together.

We were called to Boston. There would be many giants along the way, but we were not grasshoppers; we were servants and missionary warriors trusting God every step of the way.

CHAPTER 72

LEVELED AND NEW BEGINNINGS

IT HAD been many years since we drove on South River Road in Bedford, New Hampshire. There were new buildings along the way and different signs. This was the same drive we had taken for twelve years of our lives. Faith Christian Center and Faith Christian Academy had been home to us. The friends and ministry coworkers from there were a part of a treasured chapter of our lives. Our drive was full of nostalgic and sentimental feelings.

From 1985 through 1997, our lives were centered there. I taught first grade at FCA and served as an administrative assistant to Pastor John Fortin. Doug was an associate pastor and minister of evangelism. Our children went to school there, and our girls played basketball on the junior high team. Jeremy was in first grade in my classroom, the fourth room down the back hall.

Our connection with Faith Christian began in 1984 when we were building a network to establish the Crisis Pregnancy Center in Manchester. We met new friends who had a heart for pro-life issues, and many of them attended church there. Our first big step forward with the CPC was to pass out literature throughout the entire city of Manchester—to every home. It was a monumental task to take on and could only be possible with hundreds of willing volunteers from many churches. Most of them came from the FCA.

Pastor Ken was one of the main supportive pastors on the project, and his encouragement helped us reach the entire city. We became members of Faith Christian Center and served on the staff. Doug had the breakthrough of his life when Pastor Ken mandated he go for counseling. Dr. Sam Brown helped him understand what held him back in ministry settings. As a result, Pastor Ken welcomed him back to a position on the staff, and that was the beginning of years of fruitful ministry. Ken was an essential leader in our lives, and he opened doors of influence for us. He was our pastor, and he was our friend.

At the end of one of my teaching days in 1996, I stopped by the office of the church. One of the intercessors for the church was there. I always enjoyed our brief chats about what God was speaking to her concerning the ministry.

I asked her, "What has God been saying to you these days?"

Our usual conversation was lighthearted, positive, and uplifting but this was very different. She stared at me, hesitant to speak.

"Do you want to know?" she asked. I wasn't in the habit of asking questions if I didn't expect an answer, yet her demeanor concerned me.

"Of course, I always want to hear what you have to share."

She said, "The Lord is going to bring judgment to this church. This church will be humbled, but not destroyed. The building will be leveled to the ground, and there will not be one brick left on top of the other." Her words were almost whispered, and her voice was shaking. Her rosy cheeks were flushed with emotion, and tears spilled over from her eyes. She picked up a journal and read two scriptures to me: Jeremiah 49:15–16 and Obadiah 2–4.

"Now I will make you small among the nations, despised by mankind. The terror you inspire and the pride of your heart have deceived you, you who live in the clefts of the rocks, who occupy

> *the heights of the hill. Though you build your nest as high as the*
> *eagle's, from there I will bring you down," declares the Lord.*
> Jeremiah 49:15-16 NKJV

> *"See, I will make you small among nations; you will be utterly*
> *despised. The pride of your heart has deceived you, you who live in*
> *the clefts of the rocks and make your home on the heights, you*
> *who say to yourself, 'Who can bring me down to the ground?'*
> *Though you soar like the eagle and make your nest among the*
> *stars, from there I will bring you down," declares the Lord.*
> Obadiah 2-4 NKJV

I stood there for several minutes, not sure how to respond to the powerful word. "Maybe this is something you should tell Pastor Ken," I encouraged her. She assured me she had, and with her eyes closed, she sat silent.

What meaning could this have? I thought to myself. Emma was not known for overreaching or manipulating. She was a faithful, dedicated servant of the Lord.

When I told Doug about my exchange with her, he was dumbfounded too. It didn't seem to fit what we knew about the church that we loved. Our church was growing and filled with believers who were committed to Jesus. The elders were men of integrity, and we had the greatest respect for them and trust in their leadership.

We didn't share it with anyone. There seemed to be much more to the story if her message was true. While we had this information, God must have had reasons to keep us out of what was happening.

Many concerning things happened in the next year before we left to return to our roots in Pittsburgh. Doug disagreed with some of Pastor Ken's decisions. This brought about some passionate conversations and a not-so-warm goodbye when we left in July 1997.

However, our love for Pastor Ken was deep and our gratitude for his friendship and investment in our lives will always be treasured.

Hearing of Ken's unexpected death several years later broke our hearts. He had been such an important figure in our lives, and God had used him to open many opportunities for us.

After Ken's passing, the state of New Hampshire proposed building a bridge from Bedford across the river to the Manchester International Airport. The plan was to construct the bridge near the FCA property, but a surprising turn of events happened.

In the winter of 1980, a group of bald eagles returned to their nest near the Merrimack River. Faith Christian Center opened in November 1980 at the same time. The eagles were listed as endangered in New Hampshire. None had successfully produced offspring in the state for thirty years. In August 1990, the eagles fledged their first two chicks in over four decades. The new nest was built almost directly in the path of the airport access road.

The endangered eagles' protection changed the government's plan, and in 2003, the state took eminent domain and rerouted the access bridge directly through the Faith Christian Center church property. Even though the eagles never returned to the nest that changed the plan, the FCC building was completely leveled. The new access road took its place.

Ken's decisions and untimely passing brought a crisis in the church. Conflicts and several church splits all took a toll on our once-renowned church in Bedford. Many smaller congregations were birthed throughout the area, and they flourished, affecting the Greater Manchester area positively. There were broken relationships among the leaders. However, many leaders went to great lengths to make amends and forgive each other. Sadly, some of the faithful members were hurt or disillusioned by all the many challenges. They drifted away, and some walked away from their faith.

Those words that God would humble but not destroy still sat in my heart. As we drove through South River Road, I wondered at it all. Only God knows how this all fits together and I am content to trust all of it to Him and His grace, knowing that even when hard things happen there is always a redemptive work God is doing in the lives of everyone involved. I do not understand the "why," but I trust in the "who." I am grateful for the assurance that God is working, and I am so thankful for the men and women who led the way through this time, with integrity and love.

Doug pulled off the road at the access ramp. We just sat there in silence.

There was not a shred of evidence in the landscape that there had once been a building that stood as a beacon of faith to the community. We shared some memories—the worship services, mission trips, the Christmas fair, the school children playing in the parking lot, my classroom and the thousands of people who began their walks of faith in the sanctuary.

The building is gone, and the memories are in the past, yet what God did there in our lives will last forever. I had a new promise in my heart—a prayer of blessings for the many churches that started as fresh shoots from that place and a yearning for the lost sheep to find their way back to faith and restoration. I continue to carry God's heart for the restoration of God's intention for the beautiful church on the property that once brought hope and life to many. He will Himself renew, confirm, strengthen, and establish His Church—His bride.

"And after you have suffered a little while, the God of all grace, who has called you to his eternal glory in Christ, will himself restore, confirm, strengthen, and establish you."
1 Peter 5:10 ESV

CHAPTER 73

TREE HOUSE MOMENTS

"What you make of this moment changes everything. What if the path you choose becomes a road? The ground you take becomes your home. The wind is high, but the pressure's off. I'll send the rain wherever we end up."
- The Voyage, Amanda Cook.

"I GIVE UP," I mumbled in the dark as I sat in the treehouse on a raw, wintry twilight evening. Icy rain poured over me, cascading over my glasses. My red sweatshirt was soaked. I climbed up into this small hidden space to have a moment of desperation alone in my yard.

It had been eighteen months since the fire marshal of Somerville had notified us we could no longer use the ministry building to train students and house our staff. They rescinded our occupancy permit until we completed all renovations. The school leaders and students moved into a local church. Some staff moved into our home. We were living on the edge, gypsies without a home. YWAM Boston was a displaced ministry.

Several days earlier, I took a mental health break, a drive around the neighborhood, and found myself on Interstate 93 heading north. I made a quick call to my daughter.

"I thought I would drop by for a visit," I told her, no matter that the four-hour trip was not a "drop by" kind of destination. She didn't ask, but I know she wondered what state of mind I was in to "drop by."

I stopped at Walmart on the way and bought some essentials, pajamas, and a change of clothes. When she greeted me at the door, there was no mention of why I had a store bag instead of an overnight case. She didn't ask. I didn't elaborate.

That visit provided me with a break from the pressure of pioneering and looming failure. My trip back home was peaceful, filled with worship music and views of the beautiful and scenic New Hampshire countryside. I turned into the parking spot in front of my home. I sighed. I glanced at the picture window of my home. People were crowding the living room; the staff and students were all there. A flood of hopelessness came over me. How much longer could I endure the financial pressures of the remodel. How much longer would I have our staff and students taking our own living space? We had only a bedroom to call home, with people packed into every other room of our house, day and night.

I wandered past the entrance door, straight through the side yard, and climbed into the children's treehouse. I was hiding, running, and giving up.

Dramatic? Yes. That was not the first time I was tempted to give up, but it was the worst time. If we failed, all those devoted friends filling my living room would have nowhere to go, and the ministry would have collapsed.

That moment changed everything. There in the dark, I reaffirmed my commitment to the Lord.

God led us to Boston and gave us a geographic footprint for our work there. Every sacrifice was worth the dream He had planted in our hearts. The Holy Spirit met me there with hope. Faith rose in my spirit. My response to the darkness was, "My God can deliver us, but even if He doesn't, I choose to follow Him and not give in to the pressure."

My encounter in the treehouse became a marker, a reminder of God's faithful encouragement. We soon turned a corner and, within weeks, received our occupancy permit from the city and moved back into the building. Since then, hundreds of missionaries have been trained there, and tens of thousands have heard the Gospel.

The weight of accumulating trouble in your life can seem unbearable and insurmountable, and your hope disappears. Faith is impossible without hope. Focus on the mountain, and there is a mountain of despair that will try to break you.

Your response in these times will set markers that will be etched in your character, embedded in your heart, and engraved in your identity. If your eyes look to the hills where your help comes from, you will see God's purpose. Hope will rise in you as a standard of expectancy against the flood of discouragement. Strength, endurance, a willingness to engage, and a desire to proclaim your trust in God's faithfulness will flow through you.

Treehouse moments like these will define your life. He will meet you there.

Shadrach, Meshach, and Abed-Nego answered and said to the king, "O Nebuchadnezzar, we have no need to answer you in this matter. If that is the case, our God whom we serve is able to deliver us from the fiery furnace, and He will deliver us from your hand, O king. But if not, let it be known to you, O king, that we do not serve your gods, nor will we worship the gold image which you have set up."

Daniel 3:16–18

CHAPTER 74

LETTING GO AGAIN

"LET'S GO to Philadelphia," I announced with half-opened eyes before dawn had peeked over the horizon. Doug woke up to my voice, startled by the words. "What did you just say?" he asked.

My words surprised and startled me. Once the fog cleared, I realized what I had just announced and to who I had announced it. Doug was the Christian version of *Indiana Jones*.

My partner in life and ministry was always ready for the next adventure. If there is a fear gene in human DNA, God left that out of Doug's design. Our adventures had taken us to the ends of the earth, literally. Our wedding vows about sickness or health, richer or poorer, better or worse, could also have included "anywhere, anytime, by any means!"

I did vow to follow him, as Ruth said to Naomi.

> But Ruth replied, "Don't ask me to leave you and turn back. Wherever you go, I will go; wherever you live, I will live. Your people will be my people, and your God will be my God."
> **Ruth 1:16 NLT**

The Lord took me up on those words many times, and we responded to His leading. I packed my bags and called many places home in the past fifty years. We lived in homes I loved and said goodbye at times before I was ready to move on.

I decorated a farmhouse, lived in a castle in Germany, lived in our own home in New Hampshire, borrowed a flat in Amsterdam, and made a dwelling place in a tent in Athens. In eighteen months, we moved twelve times before settling down to raise our family in Goffstown.

I never really got used to letting go of home, familiar places, or the people who filled our lives in those chapters. I knew what it meant to hear God's voice and know that He had new assignments for us. Every move was both an adventure and a joy, with a side of grief from letting go.

Jesus understood the cost of leaving and gave a comforting promise to Peter.

> *"Yes," Jesus replied, "and I assure you that everyone who has given up house or wife or brothers or parents or children, for the sake of the Kingdom of God, will be repaid many times over in this life, and will have eternal life in the world to come."*
> Luke 18:29–30 NLT

He also left heaven to live on planet Earth for an eternal purpose. Every time I waved goodbye to one life to embrace a new one, I knew He was worth it and He would somehow even the scales of sacrifice, but this time was different.

Changes at twenty are exciting; changes at forty are not as much, but changes at seventy... Well, isn't this a time in your life when you get to take vacations and sip iced tea with friends, chat about family, and how great it is to not have to work so hard?

Just getting the word "Philadelphia" out of my mouth felt like a huge mistake, but the cat was out of the bag, so to speak. *Indy, who* was also known as Douglas Warren Tunney, had heard, and he was ready to go on to a new assignment.

This fateful moment happened in the fall of 2018 while we were at a YWAM conference with our Northeast bases. It was a green light for Doug, and he began to tell people. "We are thinking about Philadelphia!" I wished time had a reverse arrow or "delete this scene" button.

Several days later, I confessed my lack of enthusiasm to him. "Remember that 'Let's go to Philadelphia' moment?" He gave me the blankest stare and a slight nod. "Well, I take that back. I don't know what caused me to say that, but I am totally 100 percent sure that was NOT a message from heaven."

I have learned many things in my life about winning in a conversation. The ultimate trump and end of a conversation is "God told me!" Or "God says no." In a second, any idea of moving to Philadelphia was squashed.

I was relieved to close that door and turn the lock.

In the summer of 2019, Mark Cornacchione, the director of the YWAM Pittsburgh base and a close friend, called us. Doug had him on speakerphone. "So, in Philadelphia, a Brazilian church has property and wants to know if YWAM is interested. Do you want to look?"

Doug said, "Yes," and all the while I was shaking my head "No!"

Several weeks later, we were waiting outside the Bethel International property in Northeast Philadelphia, waiting for Pastor Paulo to show us around. The property was a former swim club that was converted into a huge house. It was a beautiful building with a guest suite, two kitchens, showers and large meeting rooms. We connected with Pastor Paulo and his wife Janet right away, and they invited us to stay in their guest room and take some time to see if God was directing us to move to Philadelphia.

We lived far away from most of our families for most of their married lives. Pioneering in Boston had been a sort of payback because our son Jeremy and his wife, Kandia, came with us, and we got to see their children regularly. Douglas and Amanda were in Asia. Rachel and Aaron were in Texas. Bethany and Chuck were in Pennsylvania. Jennifer, Evan, and Miranda lived near Pittsburgh. We missed them all the time. I wasn't open to saying goodbye to the four little Tunney girls in Boston.

During those weeks of checking out the land at the Bethel property, I was taking the Megabus back and forth to Boston. I spent one week in Philadelphia and one week in Boston.

This was another treehouse moment. Times of surrender to God's plans are hard on the heart until you can surrender to His will, remembering His faithful and loving purposes. The Joshua 4 piles of memories were reminders of God's character. I wasn't ready for a new life, yet it seemed there was one being prepared for us.

One afternoon, Doug called me at the Brazilian property. "You will never, in your wildest imagination, guess what just happened to me. My friend, Jimmy Terry, introduced me to a pastor in the northwest part of the city. Bishop Grannum and his son, Pastor Andrew, showed me an empty building, and we can have it if we will do the renovation. Remember that prayer I told you about? God, would you do the impossible and the unbelievable for the Kingdom of God and YWAM in Philadelphia? This is unbelievable."

The first time Doug brought me to the New Covenant Church campus, I thought it was a dream. The forty-four-acre property looked like a setting from Narnia. There were monumental buildings that looked like castles. It had a beautiful center field filled with towering oak trees. Eagle One was the building offered to YWAM. Bishop said, "I heard YWAM likes to fix up buildings. We have one of those."

It was a disaster. There was no heat or electricity. The plumbing didn't work. There was an industrial kitchen and an elevator, but neither worked. This abandoned building once served as the home of the Pennsylvania School for the Deaf. Doug saw it as an answer to his prayer. I saw it as a mountain that I wasn't sure we could tackle.

The potential was unbelievable, as was *what was needed* to make it livable. My administrative mind guessed it would cost us at least half a million plus labor to repair it and make it functional.

My trips to Boston ended abruptly with a ban on travel to Boston and the lockdown in Philadelphia because of COVID. The COVID lockdown gave Doug a fantastic opportunity to have a project to work on every day. Eagle One would become the home of YWAM Philadelphia.

The next eighteen months were truly unbelievable. Finances were released. After a few months, small work crews could join Doug in the renovations. Several staff members joined us. Little by little, the rooms were painted and carpeted. There was an unbelievable day when full electric power was restored, which turned on the kitchen and the elevator.

We made a home there in one wing. I live in a castle. Deer would visit our yard every evening. Little by little, my hand let go of the grip it had on my life in Boston and embraced our new home. The feelings of loss were replaced with a fresh expectation that God had a plan for us there. He always has in each new chapter.

All our previous experiences—equipping, pruning, lessons, hardships and victories—had prepared us for this moment.

This book began with a story of skipping rocks. The Master takes our lives in his grip, like well-weathered stones, and skips them across the waters of life. Each impact sends ripples to distant shores, leaving an imprint of His purpose. None of our experiences were wasted. The Lord was with us every minute of this new chapter.

A lot has changed in my life since the days when I first went off to college, angry with my circumstances and unmindful of the promises that both my mother and I had made to God in my youth. A lot has changed in Doug's life since the days when he had his life transformed and set on an alternative path. Our journey of faith and ministry has since shown me the true meaning of living for His glory.

CHAPTER 75

THE TURNPIKE

KENNYWOOD IS a historic amusement park near Pittsburgh. One of the favorite rides for children was the Turnpike. Antique-looking cars travel along a mile route over bridges and underpasses. There is a steering wheel, a gas pedal and a brake. It looks quite authentic. Young motorists have a sense of control as they drive along the trail. The actual control they have is very limited.

"Can I drive?" asked my son, jumping into the car. I nodded. In a minute, the attendant released the car that was governed by a middle track. Although the car moved on its own, my son had the pedal to the floor and was turning the steering wheel at every bend in the road. A few times along the way, he got anxious and started flailing between the brake and gas. The steering wheel was spinning around, but the car just moved steadily at a pace set out for it. The speed was controlled by a programmer who put safety limits on every move.

When we pulled into the end zone and the car stopped, my son looked up at me with a sense of pride and accomplishment.

"I am a great driver, right?"

Again, I nodded with a smile. I didn't want to break it to him that there was a bigger plan set out for his ride and that his contribution was to just get in the car and stay in the car.

Our walk with the Lord is so much like that. When we step into the car on our day of salvation, we grip our hands on the steering wheel and put our foot on the pedal. Our journey will take us through bends and tunnels and sometimes scary places, and we can think we have to take control and it is all up to us. When those anxious moments come, we need to just stay in the car. Our Father in heaven knows the path we are on, and He is there.

CHAPTER 76

LESSONS FROM THE JOURNEY

In the future, your children will ask, 'What do these stones mean?'
Joshua 4:21 NLT

THROUGHOUT this book, we have shared stories from our lives—memories, milestones, and markers that have pointed to our life's mission: **to know God and make Him known.** Along the way, we learned essential life lessons that prepared us for every new chapter. These sometimes strengthened us, corrected us, inspired us, or helped us to focus our lives. They were memorial stones to remind us of God's trustworthiness.

Often, friends and acquaintances observe our outward lives and miss the inner journey. I once had a friend tell me I had a "Clever Family," referring to the 1960s television show *Leave It to Beaver*. It shows a perfect family where everyone is well, and everything always goes smoothly.

That couldn't be farther from the reality of living for Jesus. There were challenges and detours, as well as heartbreaks, along the way. We made mistakes. We faced disappointments. We lived our lives dependent on Jesus, trusting in His character and rooted in His friendship. He promised in Jeremiah 29:13–14 that if we seek Him with all our hearts, we will find Him.

- **We found Him to be our Father** in Luke 15 when our son Brian was restored to us after sixteen years. We got to understand why heaven rejoices when one lost lamb is found. Our family experienced the profound, overwhelming joy of a father holding a son who had come home.

Family is a priority for Him. The ministry was an outgrowth of the home and was not intended to compete with the family. We established boundaries to protect our children and assure them we would always put them first. Even when the ministry or the community seemed to require our time or attention.

- **We found Him to be our Comforter** during times of grief. Some people we treasured left us too soon. We said goodbye to others too often.

I often thought about Jesus at Lazarus' tomb, weeping with Mary and Martha. He knew a shout would awaken his friend in a moment. Lazarus would be unwrapped with a new lease on life. Yet He identified with the pain of death, disillusionment, and disappointment. We felt His arms around us and His words of compassion in the most difficult moments.

- **We found Him to be our Redeemer** when He sought us out and brought us to salvation. He met me sitting in an auditorium watching "Hair" and met Doug on his knees in his bedroom. Jesus came to seek and save the lost, and there is no doubt that He came for us, relentless in his love for us.

Our lives have continued to change as we grow in our knowledge of Him. A Christian's reality is from glory to glory.

- **We found Him as our Provider** as our needs were met—from our daily bread to healing to new friends and places to call home. He showed us He knew us intimately when He provided dolls for our daughters in Greece, shoes for Doug, and when an African sailor gave us the funds to return home after our year in Europe.

We learned that the need is not the call. But where he leads, the provision will follow. On our first trip to Brazil, Earl Tygert told us, "You are trusting God for thousands of dollars for this trip; there will come a day when you trust God for hundreds of thousands to do the ministry that He will call you to!" Those words have been prophetic for our lives.

- **We found Him as our Guide,** lighting our path and showing us the next step.

We learned to hear His voice in the quiet moments. We recognized open doors, open hearts, and doors of opportunity for the Gospel. Sometimes we stepped into the unknown only to realize He had prepared the way ahead of us. A closed door opened to a different college for me, and Doug was waiting there. A closed door on the YWAM ship brought us to new adventures in Holland and Germany. We have learned to rest in God's answers to our prayers for guidance. He has always had a clear path ahead.

- **We found Him as our Counselor** when faced with conflicts with others and in our own hearts.

Living for Jesus did not insulate us from internal and external stress. The struggles purified us as the impurities in our character rose to the surface. The Lord always provided wise counselors to help us do the work of forgiving and recognizing areas in us that needed healing or deeper understanding. Pam helped me see my need to forgive my father. Dr. Sam helped Doug understand the roots of being driven in ministry. Many other friends and ministry leaders brought clarity to our conflicts and helped us grow.

ABOUT THE AUTHOR

DEBRA TUNNEY is an encourager, mentor, teacher, woman's speaker, and ministry developer. Her missionary travels have taken her to over 20 nations on 5 continents.

She is a professional educator with a B.S. in education from California University in Pennsylvania. Her ministry training has been with the University of the Nations. (YWAM)

For the past 50 years, Debra has served alongside her husband, pioneering many ministries, including *the Care-Net Pregnancy Centers in Manchester and Nashua, NH, Joshua Generation teen outreach, and the School of Evangelism and Ministry. They founded Youth With A Mission (YWAM) in Pittsburgh, Boston, and Philadelphia.*

Her passion is to encourage believers to find their God-given purpose and to help mentor young leaders to step into their calling to bring the Gospel to their generation.

3 John 1:4 "I have no greater joy than this, to hear of my children walking in the truth."

The Tunneys have four married children and 16 grandchildren. They call Philadelphia their home and current ministry calling.

Made in United States
Orlando, FL
19 April 2023